WOODSHOP LUST

AMERICAN WOODSHOPS
AND THE MEN WHO LOVE THEM

DAVID THIEL [EDITOR OF POPULAR WOODWORKING BOOKS]

POPULAR WOODWORKING BOOKS
CINCINNATI, OHIO
www.popularwoodworking.com

[READ THIS IMPORTANT SAFETY NOTICE]

Distributed in Canada by Fraser Direct
100 Armstrong Avenue
Georgetown, Ontario L7G 5S4
Canada

Distributed in the U.K. and Europe by David & Charles
Brunel House
Newton Abbot
Devon TQ12 4PU
England
Tel: (+44) 1626 323200
Fax: (+44) 1626 323319
E-mail: postmaster@davidandcharles.co.uk

Distributed in Australia by Capricorn Link
P.O. Box 704
Windsor, NSW 2756
Australia

Visit our Web site at www.popularwoodworking.com or our corporate Web site at www.fwpublications.com for information on more resources for woodworkers and our other publications.

Other fine Popular Woodworking Books are available from your local bookstore or direct from the publisher.

12 11 10 09 08   5 4 3 2 1

Library of Congress Cataloging-in-Publication Data

Woodshop lust : American woodshops and the men who love them / edited by David Thiel.
    p. cm.
ISBN-10: 1-55870-822-7 (pbk. : alk. paper)
ISBN-13: 978-1-55870-822-8 (pbk. : alk. paper)
1. Woodshops--United States. 2. Woodworkers--United States. I. Popular woodworking.
TT185.5.W66 2008
684'.08092273--dc22

2007034909

ACQUISITIONS EDITOR: David Thiel
SENIOR EDITOR: Jim Stack
DESIGNER: Brian Roeth
PRODUCTION COORDINATOR: Mark Griffin
PHOTOGRAPHER: Al Parrish, and individual authors

F+W PUBLICATIONS, INC.

[ACKNOWLEDGEMENTS]

I want to thank woodworkers in general for their amazing capacity for openness. We will talk to anyone about our hobby and share our knowledge and experience without any thought of personal gain. Some of the best people I have ever met are woodworkers.

Many thanks to the thousands of members of The Woodworker's Book Club (www.woodworkersbookclub.com) for providing the spirit to keep woodworking a growing hobby and to the dedicated woodworkers at Wood Central (www.woodcentral.com) for always being on-line with a supportive comment or a fast answer to those "dumb" questions that hit on Sunday afternoon. And a special thanks to the leader of the Wood Central pack, Ellis Wallentine, who manages to keep this unruly group of individuals in line and cordial.

David Thiel

CONTENTS

Milton Ippolito's Shop

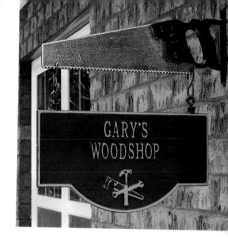

GARY'S
WOODSHOP

Gary Lytton's Shop

Rick de Roque's Shop

Ray Merrell's Shop

Woodworkers are a strange lot. Our hobby and passion is a singular, lonely activity where we will happily spend an entire weekend without saying two words to another human being. And we're happy about that. On the flip side, if a woodworker is out taking a walk and happens to notice another woodworker making dust in his garage, he won't hesitate to walk up to this stranger and say, "hello". More likely than not this chance encounter will take the better part of an hour with the two parting as old friends.

Our shops are our sanctuary, our private domain ... our Bat Cave. But we still can't wait for someone to stumble upon our secret refuge so we can show off. Sure, we want to share our completed work, but the more important part of the interaction usually centers on the woodshop itself.

We love our shops. Whether a small corner in the basement, a single car garage (where no car will ever park), or a dedicated purpose-built building complete with wood stove and refrigerator, woodworkers love their shops. We love showing them off (to anyone who will stand still long enough) and we love to see other woodworker's shops.

This book is for the woodworking voyeur who loves to peek at other woodworkers shops. We like to see how other guys work, what they've done to adapt their space to their needs, and we love to look at their tools.

For those of us who don't get out of our neighborhoods often enough, we thought it would be fun to let you (the woodworking reader) take a virtual tour of some shops from around the country.

We got in touch with some friends from The Woodworker's Book Club and from Woodcentral.com and asked if we could show off their shops. It came as no surprise that there were plenty of volunteers. Not all the shops are earth-shaking in their presentation, but each one is a shop that is loved by its woodworker. We asked the guys to show off what they're most proud of and left it at that.

We know that as you flip through these shops you'll be thinking about your own shop and saying, "Hey, my shop's more cool than that!" Good! Send me some shots of your shop (david.thiel@fwpubs. com) and we'll get started on next years' book!

Enjoy the tour, and see if you don't pick up a few ideas that you'll put to work in your shop next weekend!

David Thiel

GAR

AGE

GARAGE WOODWORKING IS A WHOLE LOT LIKE SERVING ON A SUBMARINE. IT'S TOO HOT, OR TOO COLD, WITH VERY LITTLE ROOM. THINGS ARE ONLY OUT OF STORAGE WHILE IN USE. EVERYTHING HAS A CAREFULLY PLANNED STORAGE LOCATION AND HAS TO FIT INTO EXACTLY THE SAME SPOT. IT'S A CAUTIOUS BALLET WITH SHARP TOOLS.

THERE IS, HOWEVER, A CERTAIN SATISFACTION IN KNOWING THAT YOU MANAGE TO CREATE FURNITURE IN A SPACE THAT MOST PEOPLE CONSIDER JUST STORAGE. OUR HATS OFF TO THE GARAGE WOODWORKERS THAT MAKE THE MOST OF WHAT'S AVAILABLE!

A TOUR OF DAVID THIEL'S SHOP

Maineville, OH

I've been in big shops and little shops, but this one is my smallest. In a one-car garage attached to my condo, I actually have all the tools I need. The car won't fit, but the girls' bikes do.

With a 7'-long traditional cabinetmaker's bench (left over from my father's custom woodworking company) and a hanging cabinet made from scrap sassafras and plywood, I have a comfortable little corner to work in. And, of course, Paige Davis is there to keep me company.

Over my 12 years with *Popular Woodworking* (both the magazine and now the book division) I've always had access to an embarrassing number of woodworking tools and machines, but I've always maintained a shop at home. My current one-car shop is smaller than ever, but I'm proud to say I have every tool a wood shop could need. Granted, things are tucked away until needed, and most of the tools are on casters to make movement easier, but it's all there!

The garage is wired with 110 and 220. No heat or air, but during the warmer months an open garage door and a couple of fans make things comfortable. In the winter a space heater and an extra sweatshirt do the job.

The trickiest part is where to do assembly. That's when the table saw gets a sheet of plywood on it and becomes a work surface. Lumber storage is also a little tight, so it's much more of a "just-in-time" inventory arrangement.

Yes, those are shoes hanging on the wall. About ten years ago a *Popular Woodworking* reader sent in this "drill holster" tip and I've had a wall of shoes from that day on. I still think it's a terrific idea. My goal is to have a drill for every application so I'll never have to change a bit or screw tip. Half way there!

While not the size equipment I'd love to have, a 6" jointer and 13" portable planer (with roller stand, very important for a one-person shop) can handle the great majority of woodworking tasks. A Grizzly dust collector hooks to the tool in use at the time. Conveniently, the small shop space makes it only necessary to shift the hose. And yes, there's a mortiser tucked away in the corner.

The car that doesn't fit in the garage. The sacrifices we make for our hobby. The license plate makes sure that all my neighbors know where to go to borrow a hammer, drill or whatever.

When I started planning out this garage shop I knew that storage space would be critical and tried to use every space available. Amazingly, once I had everything in the garage, I found that I had storage space that I wasn't using! Guess that means I still have room for more tools. Oh darn.

Some simple storage racks and cabinets from Lowes make ample room for all the portable power tools and more. The shop radio is perched at the ready to keep things hopping.

The 10" cabinet saw does take up a lot of room, but honestly the space is pretty comfortable. You can see the minimal lumber storage top left, and the little bit of room for sheet goods below. Of course that space is also shared with Christmas decorations. Note the planer, horses and half a dozen other tools tucked out of the way beneath the bench.

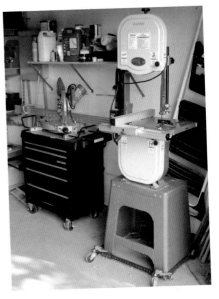

A 14" bandsaw (on wheels) and a 10" sliding compound miter saw with fence extensions (on a great rolling storage cart) share space with the "garage" storage shelf above.

With all those drills stuck in shoes, there have to be a bunch of chargers. A leftover bathroom cabinet serves as home base, and also has drawers to hold my 17 pairs of safety glasses. I'm not kidding. Guess I'm addicted.

I built this rolling cart for the magazine and couldn't part with it. It stores the majority of the small supplies, sharpening, sanding and more. Tucked behind the left door is a benchtop drill press. Behind the right door (next to the clubs) is a small combination belt/disc sander.

A TOUR OF EUGENE STERN'S SHOP

With a 20' X 20' garage, floor space is at a premium. All tools are on a mobile base. Just enough room for my 2005 Toyota pickup.

Tools take up ½ of the garage floor. The two upper cabinets are 4' high, 7' long and 32" deep! Each drawer is customized sized for the tools it houses.

The upper cabinets: Each drawer is full extension and houses specific tools.

My shop is small, being only 20' x 20', and must share space with the truck. I am an accountant by vocation and like to do some woodworking to relax. I like making furniture and doing some intarsia projects. My work shop is a work in progress. I would like to add a central dust collection system. I am in the process of remodeling my home and would like to have things in place before I retire.

Floor space is at a premium and everything must either roll to the walls or be hung up. The two main cabinets are 4' high x 7' long and 30" deep. What makes this work are the full extension drawers custom fitted for each tool or supply needs. Each drawer will have labels to be able to quickly identify the drawers' contents. The cabinets are mounted up high, about 6' off the floor, so a ladder is needed to get to cabinets.

The garage is wired with 110 and 220. All of my tools are on wheels so they can be moved out of the way at night. The cabinets are large and aren't perfect, but it's my space.

Above is my Excalibur dust collection and blade guard system mounted to a shop-built sleeve that can be raised out of the way or lowered when needed. The system is also mounted to a rail so the whole system can be moved over the table saw. At top right is my Craftsman 10" contractor saw mounted on a mobile base with table and Excalibur in place. I can make cuts up to 50" with the aftermarket edge guide attached, or using a sled, can cut longer boards or panels while at the same time giving them support.

Router workstation, combination 10" miter saw and (not shown) 13" planer. The station has wings to support longer material but are lowered in this view. To the right is my 10" radial arm saw mounted on another mobile base with storage. The cabinets above and the two drop-down shelves can hold plans or measuring tools.

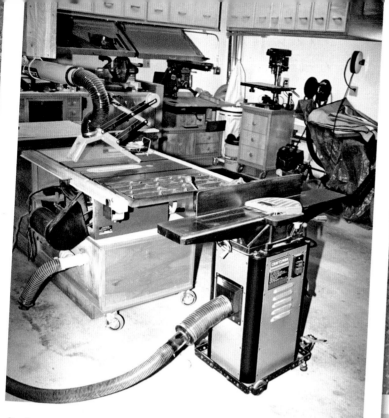

Craftsman 6" jointer and dust collection.

My scrap wood and project lumber store-all, also on wheels, so I can get to both sides.

A Noah's Ark toy chest that I built for my grandson Ethan when he was born. I purchased the plans and exotic wood kit from Cherry Tree Toys. The project took me six months to complete. The zebra alone took me a weekend to cut out, let alone sanding and fitting. The chest is made out of oak and I milled the boards myself.

An additional project I have in mind is to build a wooden strip kayak. Have never done one before, but I believe in challenges and with a little research should be able to produce a respectable boat that I will be proud to say I built it myself.

A TOUR OF RICK DEROQUE'S SHOP

Conway, AR

This is the shop. You may ask why I would use the small one car garage for my shop when I also have a two car garage. Central heat and air! The small garage is fully insulated and is part of the central heating and cooling of the house. The two car garage isn't. It gets mighty hot here in Arkansas in the summer. This is me at the door to my shop with my new apron my lovely wife made for me for Father's day. Notice the heavy-duty wheels on the 800-pound planer, they really help when moving it around.

I'm a physical pherapist and work all week with people, which I love, but it's nice to be able to work in relative solitude for a few days to recharge the batteries. I have yet to have a piece of wood say that I'm killing them or causing pain. The idea of creating something from a tree has always interested me but I've not had the opportunity until about four years ago when the kids started leaving the nest and I had the time to devote to woodworking.

I didn't think I could fit in an 11' x 22' shop much less a bunch of tools but found I was able to fit a full complement of tools as well as me. When I was setting up my shop four years ago I took the shop size as a challenge to be efficient, but not sacrifice the ability to make the kinds of furniture I wanted to make. It needed to have dust collection since our den (computer room) is right on the other side of the door and my wife would NOT be happy with the dust – and I know if she's not happy I'm definitely not happy. The family calls my dust collection system the squirrel cage. It does sound like squirrels are nesting in there at times. The 20" planer and the 8" jointer are on wheels so that when the dimensioning is done they can be moved out of the way. Since I normally only work with solid wood I didn't need to make room for big panels of sheet goods. My cabinet saw is a 3 HP 10" Grizzly that has worked well for me. I also have a floor model drill press, an 18" Jet band saw, a 6" x 48" combo sander, a router table, and a number of hand planes.

The view from the North end of the shop. I built everything so I could learn how to use the tools. The mistakes (and they were many) helped me learn a lot about using the tools. Notice the hand tools. Even with a lot of corded tools I believe a person needs hand tools to do fine work. The benches, router table, TS, and outfeed table are all the same height so nothing gets in the way and each can help support the workpiece. I put the mats down after a year of walking on the hard concrete — it has made a big difference on my feet. The workbench/outfeed table is made of four sheets of birch ply with oak trim. It's very stable, inexpensive and has worked very well.

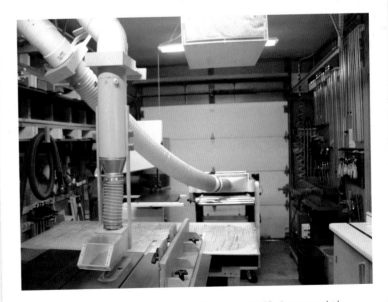

This is the South end of the shop. I have the 20" planer and the 8" jointer on wheels so I can move them out of the way when the dimensioning is done. The DC hose comes from above the planer so it doesn't interfere with the wood coming out the end of the planer.

This is the bank of drawers under my utility workbench. These hold most of my smaller tools, sharpening stones, etc. The smaller bank of drawers on the right hold smaller items like loose screws. My wife says I have a screw loose, so now she knows where to find it.

PAPA'S WOODSHOP
Personal, financial, gardening, car and household advice given upon request.

My daughter Allison made this for me, she is so nice. But when she was a teenager I don't think she thought this highly of my advice.

I remember when I got my No. 60½ low-angle block plane tuned just right and called my wife to the shop to show her how well it worked. I took some wisps of shavings and looked up waiting for the oos and ahs but she had this look on her face like, "OK, now what?" Some people just don't understand.

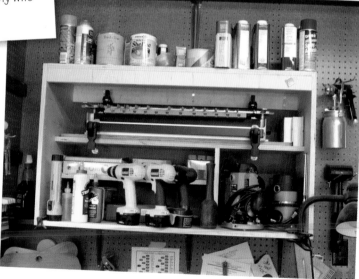

It doesn't look like much but it does the job. Nice place for the D4, easy to get to but out of the way. When I first started the shop I had a chance to get two routers at a very good price but bought only one because I thought "what would I need more than one router for?" I now have five routers and feel I NEED each one.

I don't have a lot of land but I work in a rural area and friends have allowed me to cut down some walnut, cherry, ash, and oak trees and get them milled at a local saw mill. The hard part was talking my lovely wife into letting me stack and sticker the wood in the backyard – three different times! But the fun of being able to take it from tree to finished piece is immensely gratifying.

The stack of lumber outside (above left) is oak and walnut. When that was done drying I had to make a garden for my wife in exchange for letting me dry it in the backyard. Negotiations are the key to a happy marriage.

Above is a stack of cherry, ash, and walnut with a stack of walnut burl. The wife said as long as I kept it on my side of the garage it was OK with her. My car hasn't seen the inside of the garage in years.

This lumber rack is for projects coming up. I store most of my lumber in the other garage and since it isn't insulated the lumber needs to acclimate to the shop. I built this for the wood for the next project or two. So when I get to the next project the wood is ready to be worked.

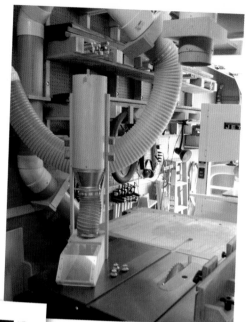

At left is the blade guard with DC. It's made of Lexan for protection. It is adjustable and can be removed with three hand screws. With it and the TS fence removed, I then have a larger area to do glue ups. This is the blade guard removed. With the hand screws, took less than a minute to do. The jig on the TS fence is from the book *Table Saw Magic* and has worked well. With the blade guard, feather boards, and splitter on the zero clearance plate I feel a lot safer. Keeps my hands away from the blade.

This is the cheap version of the more expensive ROS with DC. Did I mention I'm cheap? I had the shop vac and the ROS so I bought the good hose and put a HEPA filter on the shop vac and it does remarkably well. This is one of the better things I've done. Gets the small dust at the source.

For the most part I don't use pre-made plans because I enjoy all the processes that go into making something. This includes the design elements – picking the wood, deciding the joints needed, and the size and finish needed for the project. Since I cut and dry all my own wood, part of the fun is going through the wood pile to find just the right piece. I will sometimes take a few hours or days to choose just the right wood for the drawer fronts and my wife will wonder if I'll ever get anything built.

You can never have too many clamps. There have been projects that I have used most all these clamps. I really like the Besseys. Had to tell my wife that Besseys are not women but clamps.

I like to design the furniture I make. I'm not very good at it, but I enjoy it none the less. It's like golf where you don't have to play like Tiger Woods to enjoy the game. Now, it would be A LOT more fun if you could play like Tiger, but you get the point. I hope that as I complete each project that I will get better at all aspects of furniture making. Woodworking to me is very personal and I probably put more of myself into each project than I thought I would when I starting this hobby. But I love every minute of it.

The walnut chest of drawers (top) shows that big things can come out of small shops. It's solid walnut with ash as the secondary wood and has a solid walnut panel back. At left are a couple of walnut night stands that are part of the bedroom set I'm making. It goes with the walnut chest of drawers.

Here I am, the proud owner of a small shop. As you can see, my shop is small, one bay of a three car garage. It's great when the weather is nice and I can open the door and enjoy the outdoors and the light. During the winter, with the door closed, it can feel more like a cave. But that doesn't stop me from being out there.

Although small, the shop is efficient. Everything is portable. All the equipment is on wheels for repositioning. And the wall mounted organizers are hung on cleats and can be repositioned as equipment is moved around. I've always heard you can never have too many clamps, but the real challenge is to find enough wall space to hang them.

I've often been accused of being a little anal about my tool/shop organization. My daughter's favorite past time is to rearrange the tools on my bench just to aggravate me. I don't understand her sense of humor.

I am an engineer for a manufacturing company in Tulsa but in my free time I'm an amateur woodworker. There is nothing more relaxing to me than to spend time in the shop (although free time is becoming increasingly hard to find).

I am relatively new to woodworking, having been at it for only about two years now. I have learned my hobby by building jigs, fixtures, and storage units for the shop. With every organizer or storage unit I build I try to incorporate different joining techniques and features. My family and friends began asking if I was ever going to build anything other than jigs and fixtures so I had to finally move on to some more challenging furniture projects. I still get some of my greatest enjoyment from adding to the shop.

As you can see from the photos, most of my equipment comes from Grizzly tools. Grizzly has a warehouse in Springfield, Missouri, which is about a 2-1/2 hour drive from my house. I use this distance as an excuse to bring home a pickup load on every visit ("Really honey, I need to bring home two or three tools to make the trip worthwhile").

Did I say it was in one bay? Well, except for what overflows into the next bay. My wife has made it clear that my car will be the first to be parked outside if I encroach any farther into her side of the garage. Maybe she'll trade the two car side for my one.

Looking from the second bay into the first. Yes, "Cold Beer" does get tested here, and tested, and tested...

My magazines and books are stored in an otherwise unused area above the door. I keep waiting for this to fall under the weight. Looks like I'll need to expand this unit soon.

Obviously every flat surface needs to be used in a small shop. My table saw doubles as an assembly table when not in use. I have also inset a router table between the rails to save space.

All drawers were designed and built utilizing removable dividers so they can be easily reconfigured as I add to my tool collection. Remember, every new project should require a new tool.

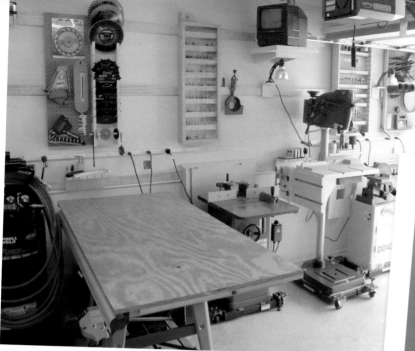

Many of the wall-hung organizers shown here were recreations from plans in various magazines and woodworking books. I usually take creative license in adapting them to my particular needs (or moods). Obviously, the shop is a work-in-process — as it should be.

Note the ingenious (at least I thought it was at the time) use of mailing tubes for dowel rod storage.

Smaller tools are stored within easy reach and set up as needed. I use a flat shelf which I pull out from under my miter-saw station to position the planer when needed. The shelf is on drawer slides.

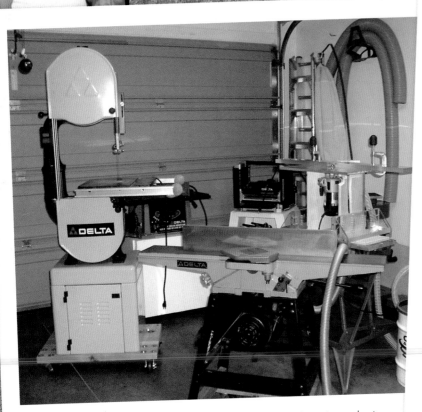

This is the equipment that made the desk, that won the prize... plenty of space until the prize equipment arrives. I'll be adding a 12" Dewalt sliding mitre saw; left-tilt hybrid 10" Delta table saw; 6" jointer; floor model drill press; and 13" planer. Thanks Minwax, and I am entering the contest again for 2007.

This was the grand prize winner in the 2006 Minwax Fall Finish Spectactular in Canada. It was made out of hickory and walnut. Both were resawn and planed to ¼" for the back and side panel inserts. The drawer sides are ¾" hickory dovetailed to the walnut drawer fronts. The tambour is made out 1" hickory and walnut strips, glued and stapled to canvas. The instructions are originally from *Mission Furniture: How To Make It*. Popular Mechanics Company, 1909.

As you can see in two photographs of my shop, it is capable of holding two vehicles. If the weather is nice, I move the dust collector outside along with whatever equipment is required for the task at hand. I will work outside even if the temperature is around 25 degrees F. for short periods of time. Other than sawing with the table saw and or the band saw, all the equipment can be used inside using the filtration, collector and the vacuums. I retired in 1995 and have been working on wood projects seriously for about six years. They include a dresser, TV stands, cedar chests, bookshelves, and presently kitchen/china/buffet cabinets about 8' long by 7' high. The highlight of all my projects is my roll top desk completed last year in hickory and walnut.

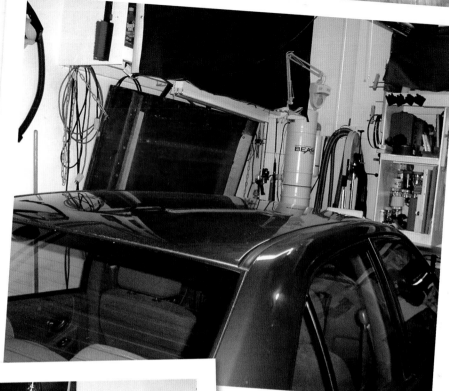

The two pictures on this page show that all this equipment, WHEN NOT IN USE and placed properly, still allows two vehicles to be parked. In front of the car is a mammoth oak typesetting cabinet used for the storage of many small hand tools, sandpaper, etc. Woodworkers never have enough storage.

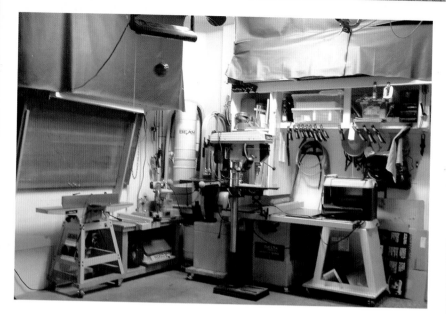

Where's the workbench? There it is, hanging on the wall, an old drafting table that drops into place (below) to make a great workbench. Above the table you see black naughyde that covers shelf space to try and keep dust out. You might ask me "Why not wooden cabinet doors? You're a woodworker." These are 5'- to 8'-foot shelving sections. For $50 and three hour's time the job is done. Time is valuable.

everything looks so clean! It is my understanding, that once the lungs are filled with sawdust, you do not have any room left to breathe, so forget the cool ale at the end of the day. So work SAFELY. That means ear, eyes and lungs.

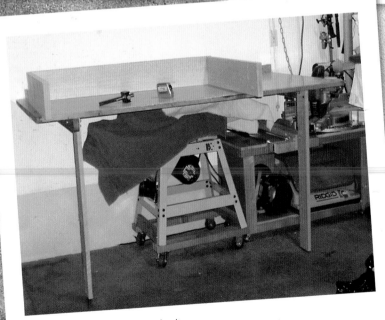

The beginning of a new project.

Almost as portable as a laptop! All the power equipment is on rolling cabinets with storage underneath.

The heart of the small tool storage. On top of the bench and above the bench is an Oak Park router table, routers, Skil saw, sanders and many other tools common to woodworking.

Depending on the urgency to finish a project, I will work maybe 4-6 hours a day. But the old adage of "Never put off 'til tomorrow, what you can do today" is sometimes translated into "Put off today what you can do tomorrow".

The kitchen unit breaks down into five units of which three are the top glass units, the bottom two units and six panels. The backs of the top unit are mirrored and the french glass finishes the doors. The only outside work was the door frames and the harvest style chair. Oak and walnut are the primary materials with a little hickory and ash.

BASE

MENT

BASEMENT WOODWORKING USUALLY (NOT ALWAYS) OFFERS MORE SPACE THAN GARAGE WOODWORKING. YOU ALSO HAVE THE BENEFIT OF HEAT AND AIR CONDITIONING. BUT IT'S NOT ALL PEACHES AND CREAM. MOVING LUMBER IN AND FURNITURE OUT OF A BASEMENT CAN BE A NIGHTMARE. YOU MAY FIND YOURSELF LONGING FOR A GARAGE DOOR. THEN THERE ARE THE INEVITABLE LEAKS, LACK OF EXTERIOR LIGHT AND THE EXTRA "COMPANIONS" – SPIDERS, CRICKETS – YOU NAME IT. FOR ALL THE BASEMENT WOODWORKERS, WE SALUTE YOU AND RECOMMEND HITTING THE TANNING BED OCCASIONALLY.

All the ideas for the shop came from magazines and books. My granddaughter (Mikayla) likes to come down and assist when she comes over.

A TOUR OF BOB PACCAGNELLA'S SHOP Menomonee Falls, WI

The storage room is ideal for the stereo and cutoffs that I can't seem to part with.

I am 47 and began woodworking in 1999 after a carpenter friend of mine brought me a radial arm saw to cut 2x4s in the garage. I learned the whole craft by reading books and never had any kind of training in school. With only that saw and a few other tools, I set up shop in the furnace room of the basement of my 1500 sq. ft. ranch because it was too cold outside during the winter months. After acquiring more tools, I soon found out that assembling anything in a 14' x 16' room with tools wouldn't work, and my wife reluctantly agreed to let me take over half of the basement.

My current shop is 20' x 18' with a 5' x 11' storage room for cutoffs and clamps. I like the idea of a climate controlled area with toilet and water nearby. Dust throughout the house is not a problem because we don't have cold air returns in the basement.

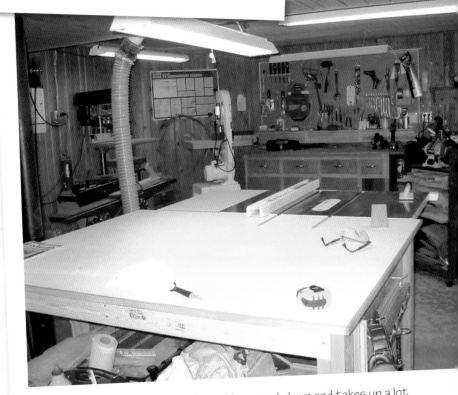

My table saw outfeed table is adjustable up-and-down and takes up a lot of valuable room. But it's invaluable for project assembly.

35

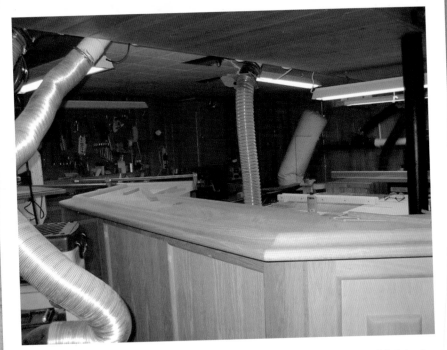

The only hassle about a basement shop is getting the wood down and finished projects up. If it's too big, I break it down and reassemble it where it goes.

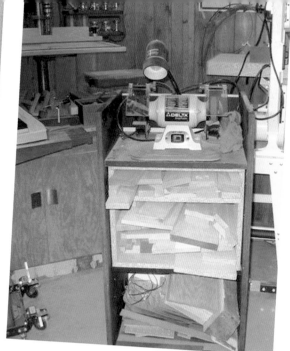

I like to recycle as many things as possible. Here is an old stereo cabinet on casters for my grinder and cutoffs. The cabinets are from a kitchen and bathroom remodel.

Now that the bedroom furniture, armoires, bars and cabinet projects are completed, I think I'll concentrate on small speaker boxes, or even better... stamp holders!

A bar I made for my brother. It was done in three sections so I could get it out of the basement. Trying to assemble the bar with limited space was a challenge.

The Steelcase file cabinet was acquired by a neighbor. It houses router tools, magazines and miscellaneous supplies.

My uncle gave me this 1950 Craftsman scroll saw — it's cast iron and heavy — but it works great!

An air filtration system made from an old squirrel cage furnace fan picked up at the local heating and cooling shop.

To take best advantage of my limited workspace, I make sure my tools all have a permanent home and they get returned to their spot when I'm done using them. Here is a view into my shop from the entrance, showing my DeWalt table saw, Rigid band saw and Delta air filter.

A TOUR OF JACK TURK'S SHOP Liberty, MO

When I retired eight years ago (I'm 75) I set up shop in the basement of our town home. You can see the heating ducts and furnace in some of the photos. It's a little crowded but I've managed to fit everything in that I need except for a jointer – and I'm working on that! I made both work benches and the two-tone cabinets you see. Since setting up the shop, I've made birdhouses, plant stands, cradles, tables and cabinets for family and friends.

Looking out from my shop into our home office. You can see the furnace to the left and my built-in miter saw on the right wall.

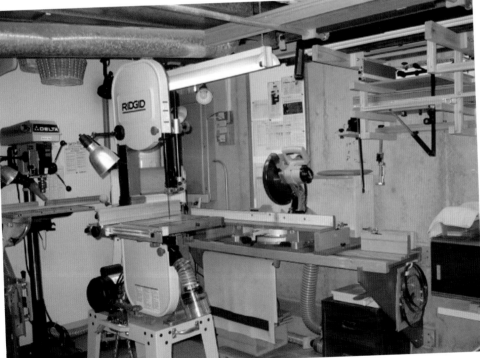

The miter saw and drill press are fixed along two adjacent walls, along with shelves for jigs. The thickness planer and the band saw are both on mobile bases so they can be moved around easily when I'm ready for them.

When we remodelled the basement for the workshop, we added extra circuit boxes to handle the demand for additional lighting and provide easily accessible outlets for power tools. I use both fluorescent and task lighting in my work area.

This workbench was my first project in building the shop. The tool board gives me easy access to frequently used tools and gadgets. It has task lighting at each end and power tools stored on the lower shelf.

My dust collector helps keep the air clean and I use the overhead beams to hang gloves and several spot lights that I use primarily on finishing projects. My router table (center) is kept covered when not in use for additional work surface.

The copier stand has a pull-out tray for easy access to the shredder and a shelf for extra work surface. I included shelves for storage of paper and supplies. It is also made of oak plywood and finished with polyurethane.

This built-in cabinet wraps around the file cabinets in our home office. It's made of oak plywood with solid oak trim and counter and is finished with three coats of wipe-on polyurethane.

Clamps are stored in a convenient corner near the work bench.

Woodworking Hobbits and job shoppers think circular. My home basement hobby shop layout is wonderfully circular. The center of the circle is the workbench. All my furniture, craft, and home improvement projects are one-of-a-kind products, not lending to a production type of layout. After each milling operation, I would typically find myself back at the workbench to check a measurement, do a hand tool operation with a chisel or plane, check a fit with a mating part, or perform a dry-fit assembly operation.

My shop has two requirements of portability and dust collection. All large power tools, benches, tables, and cabinets ride on wheels. I can easily move the 12'- long CMS or RAS work station by myself. Every power tool is connected to the vacuum dust collection system. The collection system works well enough to allow time to save for a dream air dust collection system.

Heaven must have a workshop ... Or is heaven in my workshop? Yea, here or there, I am in heaven.

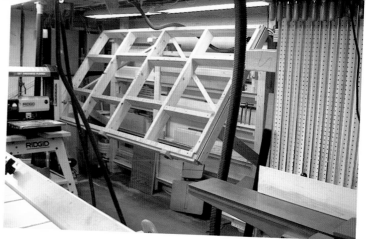

This is my dimensioning station and wood storage area. The dimensioning station consists of a panel cutoff table, an 8" jointer and a 13" planer. The panel cutoff table is shown in the cutting position, adjusted 35° off the wall. The construction of the panel table is that of an open sided torsion box. It will hang horizontally from the ceiling for easy access to the storage shelves behind it. Cutoffs are stored on the 8" shelf. The table also hangs vertically to open up a 5' x 10' area in front of it, useful for temporary storage or alternate assembly area. The ply, lumber and jig storage is hidden behind the white peg board clamp rack, shown in the right hand corner.

For glue-ups, I attach a glue-up clamp rack to the table. The table is ideal for dimensioning ply and large items like 26" taper cuts, which would require a jig on the TS and is too long for a RAS cut.

The wet-and-dry sharpening station is on the outer circle, where the occasionally used tools reside.

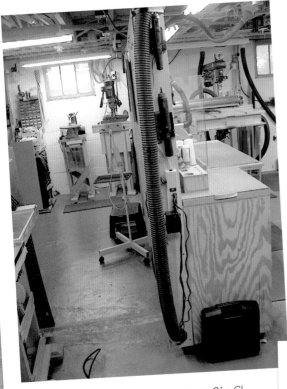

The mortising and drilling stations are right of the scroll and jig station.

Behind the RAS station, there is an 8' x 6' open space assembly area, the future home for a height-adjustable torsion-style assembly table. Moving Northwest is the scroll and jigsaw station at the far end of this picture.

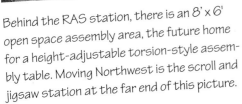

To be productive it's important to locate hand tools and accessories quickly, and to have clutter-free work stations. Everything has its home. Before leaving the shop, dust and tools are properly stored.

The workbench, shown above, is on fold-away wheels and features dogs, T-track for hold down clamps, adjustable end stop, side stop, tool tray with cover, and two vises.

The CMS workstation provides peg hangers for tools, measuring instruments, and other accessories. The top edge is a clamp rack. Also, its table top has a track with tape measure and stops; providing for repeatable precision cutoffs. The open cabinets make it very quick to retrieve portable power tools, chisels, and other items. It serves my short-term memory well as a continual reminder of where things are stored.

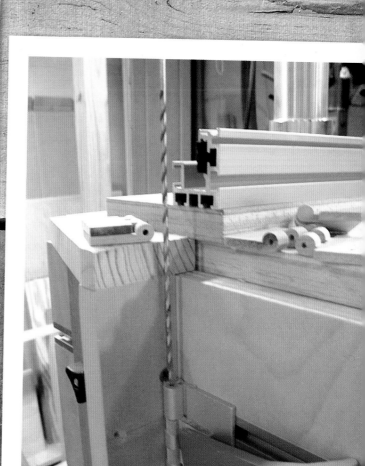

This picture shows the RAS work station, also with open cabinets, pegboard hangers, and clamp rack. Like the CMS station it has a dust collection shroud. The RAS table has an imbedded steel bar grid to keep it flat. The RAS station includes a dust free battery charging station that contains three battery chargers.

The radial drill press utilizes a horizontal and vertical table combination (see first picture, far left). The top table has a sacrificial cutout and a split fence inclusive of a tape measure guide. The fence slides forward in a T-track that also includes two tape measure guides. Upper and lower dust collection is included. The vertical table has an adjustable fence and T-track for clamping.

The dust shroud shown in place on the radial arm saw.

Under the TS/RT is a 22" drawer blade cabinet, which contains all my 7", 10", 12" and dado blades and safety devices.

My shop is my haven. It's taken years of enjoyment putting it all together. As you can see, I purchase moderately priced tools, restore old tools and build some, like the down-draft table. All approaches are part of a fun hobby. Old hand tools are great finds at auctions and flea markets. I really enjoy the nostalgic feeling when using them.

46

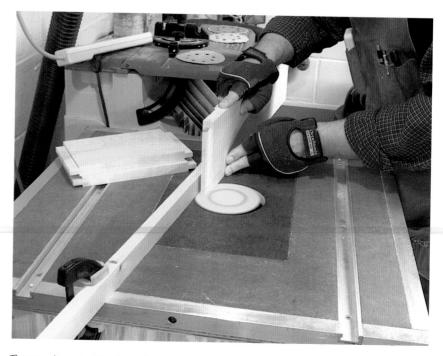

The sanding station includes my concept of a sanding down draft table that houses the sander. It's shown in use here. No roundover or divots with this unit. The ROS or belt sander can mount into this down draft table.

I like learning new techniques. The four boxes at left are done with a Porter Cable dovetail jig. The (center, rear) sea chest was made with a shopmade box joint jig. The center jewelry box with an Incra jig. The candle box was done with the band saw and hand chisel. The other two are band saw boxes.

My daughter Kayse requested a gate leg table with high stool seating. I designed it with a Shaker influence and touch of fair curve in the gate leg. My wife Cheryl and son Kelly also benefit from my hobby shop. Kara, my oldest daughter, is a woodworking artist and makes furniture for me.

Before I had a finishing room, I stuck to hand rubbing tung oils, shellac, and extra thinned varnish. Now with the finishing room I can spray and better control dust and odors.

This here is the workhorse of the shop. My table saw and router setup. I've extended the router table and put in a miter track, which helps support wider material. Notice the exercise mats on the floor — sure helps when chisels and sharp tools are dropped — not to mention the knees.

My name is Ken , and I've been woodworking since the seventh grade. It was put on hold while I was in the Air Force for six years. After working on nuclear submarines at a naval shipyard, I've retired and that gives me plenty of time to do woodworking. It's my favorite hobby and pastime. For a long time I had all these tools in a 360 sq. ft. garage while living in California. Recently I've moved to Colorado, and my basement shop has more than doubled in size — I love it. I'm still in the process of putting it together. I've just survived my first winter with little heat in my basement, so I recently installed a gas fired stove. Now my cut lines should become straighter in the winter.

I like to build a variety of projects. I've made toys for underprivileged kids during Christmas. My favorite woodworking is Intarsia. Some of them include a cub/bear, clown, and bass. I'm working toward selling some projects in a local gift shop. My new adventure will be trying my skills at the art of inlaying.

As you can see, my shop consists of many different hand and power tools. A collection of many years. Plus, once I worked in a tool store and got all tools at ten percent over cost, so I couldn't help from buying more tools. And my wife asks, how many saws can one woodworker have, and I reply never enough. I tell the wife every tool has it's function, I think I have her convinced, as long as I keep making things for her. Most recent purchase is a Makita sliding compound miter saw, for which I still need to make support wings and bench, great tool. My next addition will be a permanent dust collection system. So, for all you woodworkers, get in your shop and make good projects happen!

This is where I carve and sand pieces of wood for the Intarsia projects I make, using my Dremel tool. It's good for rouging-out pieces, then I take them to a 220-grit flap sander. The storage racks above my bench holds small pieces of wood, brads, screws and parts. My bench top is made from a solid-core door. I have a JDS air filtration unit hanging above my table saw, that really clears the air fast. It's one of my latest additions to the shop. The shelving on the right holds most of the power hand tools, close at hand to the workbench.

I use a metal plate on the fence for a magnetic hold down and a feather board. Wood doesn't have much of a chance to kick back. The Incra 2000 miter gauge is a nice addition to the table saw, and I'm using a Forrest Woodworker II blade.

A TOUR OF TERRY ELFERS' SHOP

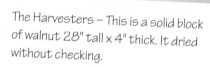

The Harvesters – This is a solid block of walnut 28" tall x 4" thick. It dried without checking.

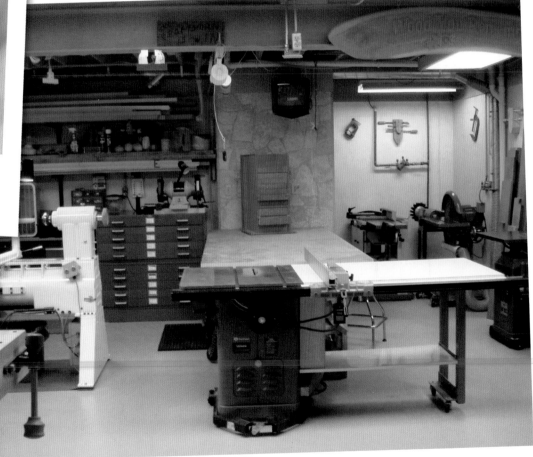

Just about everything in my shop is mobile. The cupboard behind the TV set houses the Dust Boy dust collector. The 8' long runoff table also doubles as a workbench, wood storage below, and hides the 220 wiring and duct work to the saw. Dust collector remote control hangs from the ceiling right over the saw.

The studio houses catalogs, small parts, work in progress, Hegner scroll saw, photo box, and storage for Performax drum sander.

My Oneway 2436 lathe. An old blueprint cabinet holds all kinds of tools. A shop-made tool holder rides on the lathe bed.

We built our house in 1986 and immediately began finishing part of the lower level for a family room, and the other half for my workshop. I have been interested in woodworking since I was a kid. Long ago, I started taking sculpture lessons. Since retirement, I got serious about woodturning. My wood collection is rather extensive, with over twenty species in stock.

The dusty corner contains the Grizzly spindle sander, Enco 20" disc sander, Bridgewood drum and flap sander, and the Mini Max 13" planer/jointer.

The wood room is about 12' x 12' and holds my supply of dry boards. This is one of two aisles.

A TOUR OF WALT GRANNEN'S SHOP

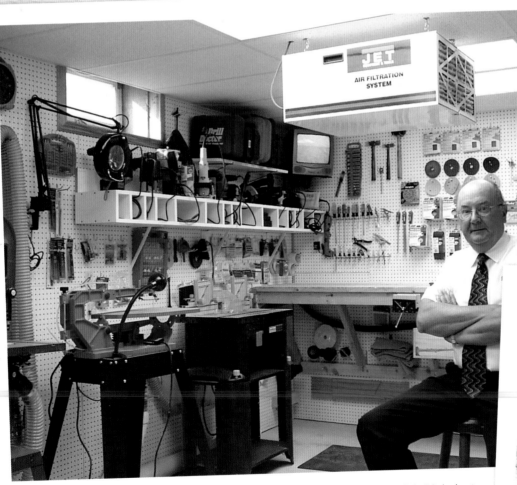

Me sitting in my shop. Over my right shoulder is my sanding bench (and the TV). With dust control being the worry that it was, I went with a JET filtration unit in the sanding area. You would have to be 6' 5" tall to hit your head on the airborne filtration, as I had our home built with a tall basement. In the picture to the right is my faithful shop dog, Maggie.

Looking Northwest at the hand held power tools; you can see how I have them organized. I abhor loose electrical cords, and I had seen a similar rack system for power tools in some- one else's shop. In my opinion, it's one of the better things I did in the shop.

I started woodworking when some friends of mine had their first baby in 1997. I wanted to build a rocking horse, so I bought some plans, some power tools and went to work in my garage. Like many of you, I grew tired of the hassles of working in a garage and the expense of trying to heat it in Wisconsin. It took some time to con- vince my wife that having my shop in the base- ment would not pollute the house with a foot of dust a week, but I got the OK to construct one.

When I was in the design stage, I knew I did not want a large shop, (did not want to clean more than would be necessary). I had it in mind if I laid it out well, and got it organized, it did not have to be large to do what I do. I decided white peg board would brighten it up in addition to being practical.

Some friends helped with the construction and wiring and, before long, I had a finished shop that measures 15' x 25'. While not large enough for building cabinets, it's large enough to build rocking toys, small projects, and pen turning.

In the Southwest corner is the band saw (on wheels), drill press and pen turning area. The hose on the right side of the picture is hooked up to the vac system and can reach any point in the shop.

53

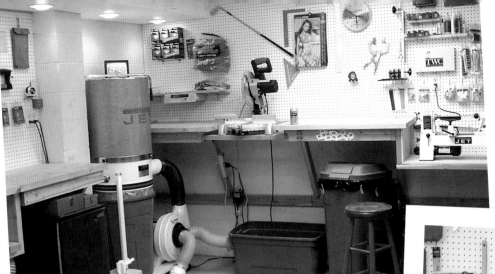

On the South wall, left to right, is my Jet canister vac, compound miter saw and pen area. The saw is situated level with the table, and located on wood dowels for easy removal and set up when a remote work site is required. Research told me it would be worthwhile to filter to 2 microns as opposed to 20 microns with the bag system. So far, it works very well. I have 4" PVC going in both directions. I had every intention of grounding it, but didn't, and I have not had a static or clogging problem. The remote starter was worth the extra money.

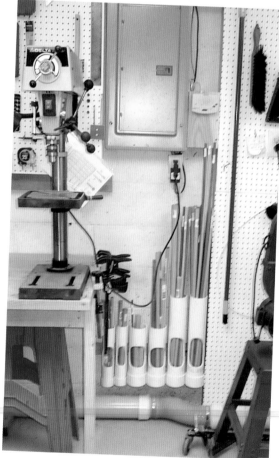

PVC tubing with a cut out for fingers, makes a nice storage rack for dowel rods.

For Christmas last year, I made six chairs for friend's grandchildren. It was almost as much fun giving them as making them.

On the East wall are my air tools, profile sander and 12" disc sander. Under the disc sander, you can see the shelves I made for holding my patterns. They pull out for easy retrieval. To the right of the profile sander, and under the bench (just barely visible) you will see a temperature controlled storage space for 12 ounce beverage cans. This comes in handy during both planning, and admiring. Looking Northeast (photo at left) is where I store my smaller items, along with my project board.

Walter Grannen Jr., printer, Army veteran

Above that table is an area for visitors to 'leave their mark in the shop'. I also keep an antique 'Calamity Jane' putter with a hickory shaft (above) and a reminder of my father, his WWII map case (photo at right).

A TOUR OF JIM STACK'S SHOP

Cincinnati, OH

I know what you're thinking — what a mess! Well, several years ago I decided that a messy shop is a busy shop. Every tool does have its place but most of the time they aren't there because I'm using them. This is about as organized as it gets.

This is my basement and it's seen a lot of years of woodworking. The walls catch dust and I'm usually too busy to get it all cleaned up. A bench top lathe sits on top of one of my most used tools in the shop – my router table. On the wall you see about one-fourth of all my clamps. As you should have guessed by now, the rest are in use on a project.

I've found that woodworkers are a very independent and creative bunch of folks. We work wherever we can find space, no matter what the surroundings. I'm lucky. With the exception of a washer, dryer and our cat's litter box, the basement is my territory. Over the past twenty-seven years that I've lived in my house and had a shop in my basement and garage, I've built scores of projects, some too large to get out of the shop without removing the door jamb (but that's another story). So, now I build smaller projects, like guitars. When I finish them, it's a simple matter to carry them upstairs.

My miter saw is mounted on an old countertop taken from a hospital remodeling demolition. This saw has seen a lot of use and just keeps on cuttin'.

My first band saw I built from a kit about 25 years ago. It's still in use in a friend's shop. Then I acquired a 60 year old band saw that I reconditioned and used for about 18 years. I purchased this band saw about three years ago and I love it. The disc sander is a 3-phase unit that I run on 220 volts single phase. I use two of the motor's three power legs. I tickle the third leg using some power from one of the other legs to get the motor up to speed, then I shut off the power to that third leg and start sanding.

I've got two areas to my shop. One is my basement, which you see in all these photos. The other is in my garage, which is connected to my basement by a man door. I have a 3hp table saw, a 15" plane and an 8" jointer in the garage, which I call my dirty room (yeah, I know, how could it be dirtier than my basement). I installed this air filter unit about a year ago in my basement and I run it constantly while I'm working. It keeps the air clean and constantly circulating. I attached it to the floor joists under my dining room.

I used to run my own furniture-making shop. This was the first thing I built – a torsion-box bench. I've laid up thousands of square feet of veneer using this table. It also works great for making chairs because it's got a perfectly flat top. All I have to do is sit the chair I'm making on this bench top and cut the leg that is too long to match the others.

The garage part of my shop is a cave. Three walls and the ceiling are concrete. As a result, I have a lot of cave crickets that live in it. They're harmless and constantly keep an eye on me.

My toolbox has lots of small drawers that hold a lot of stuff. It's amazing really. I can put tools in it and not remember where I put them for weeks.

STALL

WOODWORKERS WHO ENJOY THE BENEFITS OF A STAND ALONE SHOP ARE LIVING IN THE LAP OF LUXURY! ADEQUATE SPACE FOR ALMOST ANY WOODWORKING TASK (OFTEN CUSTOM BUILT TO THEIR NEEDS), WINDOWS, EASY ACCESS AND USUALLY HEAT AND AIR CONDITIONING! WE ALL KNOW IT COMES AT A REAL COST, BUT DEEP DOWN IN OUR HEARTS, IT'S WHAT ALL WOODWORKERS DREAM OF. CONGRATS ON ACHIEVING YOUR DREAM!

ND

ONE

A TOUR OF BRIAN COE'S SHOP

My four-year old son David enjoys sweeping up shavings, playing with his hammer and nails, etc. He's posing with two scroll saws, (one restored and one as-found), that are early examples of the first tools manufactured by the company that became the famous Delta brand of power tools.

Here I am with two of my dozen (nope, not a typo) band saws. Why so many? I guess you could say my motto when it comes to machinery is to "change tools, not tooling." The little bench top Delta was the first power tool I ever bought. I still keep it set up with a 1/8" blade for delicate inlay and scrollwork. It's sitting on the table of my favorite band saw, a Moak Super 36 direct drive saw. The saw has a 36" throat, with a 24" resaw capacity under the blade guides, and takes a blade just shy of 20'. At 9' tall and 2,500 pounds, it's rock steady and can handle anything from scrolling out bracket feet to resawing the largest timbers. The mobile base for this saw is a two-ton pallet jack.

This combination of a MiniMax 24" band saw and MiniMax FS350 14" jointer/planer make for a great ripping and resawing lane. Four sanding tools (edge sander, oscillating spindle sander, 12" disk sander, and 18" drum sander) are visible on the wall behind them. To the right of the jointer/planer is a Delta 16½" variable speed drill press.

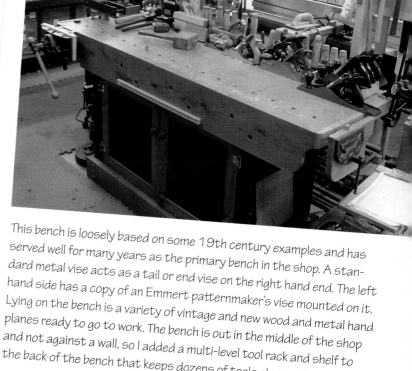

This bench is loosely based on some 19th century examples and has served well for many years as the primary bench in the shop. A standard metal vise acts as a tail or end vise on the right hand end. The left hand side has a copy of an Emmert patternmaker's vise mounted on it. Lying on the bench is a variety of vintage and new wood and metal hand planes ready to go to work. The bench is out in the middle of the shop and not against a wall, so I added a multi-level tool rack and shelf to the back of the bench that keeps dozens of tools close at hand.

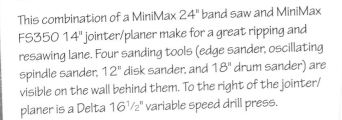

I'm a museum director in public programming and education at an 18th century living history site. I am fortunate enough to get to examine a lot of early American furniture, particularly pieces made in the South. Not surprisingly, my main interest is in period reproductions and new interpretations in the styles of the 18th and 19th centuries. As a result, my shop relies heavily on hand tools for joinery, details, and final work, and larger machinery for processing wide and thick hardwoods. Actually, most of my early training and woodworking was all done with hand tools using 18th century techniques. True to my historical interests, the majority of the larger machinery is of vintage design from the 1950's and 1960s that has been restored or is in the process of being restored. Currently, my shop is a pole building with wood siding and metal roof, 28' x 36'. A separate metal building stores lumber.

In the last several years my shop and interest in period furniture has turned into a sideline business, allowing me to earn extra income for the shop while producing period reproductions for other museums and individuals. I've even had a chance to make some props for a couple of well-known Hollywood movies that required period items. (Mel Gibson's The Patriot and Russell Crowe's Master and Commander.)

Here is a photo of me in my shop with an example of the period furniture work that I tend to do. This is a circa 1820s walnut desk and bookcase from rural NC. It contains several "secret" compartments, and is awaiting the restoration glass for the bookcase doors and its writing lid on the desk. Behind me are some of the antique molding planes used to construct my pieces authentically, and in front on the assembly table are some of my bench planes.

Here is a close up of some of the bench planes used daily in the shop. There are some antique English infills, a modern Lie-Nielsen, and several Continental style carved and inlaid wooden planes I have copied after 18th century originals.

If one is good, two must be better! The Delta Unisaw is the classic 10" cabinet saw. This pair from 1956 and 1968 shares a common dust collection and a single fence rail. The one on the left is set up with a crosscut blade, aftermarket miter gauge, and miter gauge extension to do joinery cuts. The right hand saw is dedicated to a dado blade for doing rabbits, dadoes, and other heavy stock removal jobs.

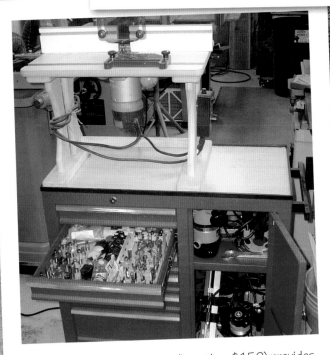

This inexpensive router setup (less than $150) provides me with as much storage and flexibility as many expensive commercial setups. It provides shelves and drawers for storage of routers, router sub bases, wrenches, collets, fences, and dozens of bits. And it's mobile too!

These two rolling clamp carts provide storage for over 450 clamps and take up less than 15 square feet of floor space, and since they roll and swivel, all of the clamps are easily accessible. The drill press shown is an example of the 1960s Unidrill by Delta Rockwell. When I acquired it to restore, it had been sitting unused for several years and a mouse had filled the quill spindle and head casting with his nest and seed storage!

65

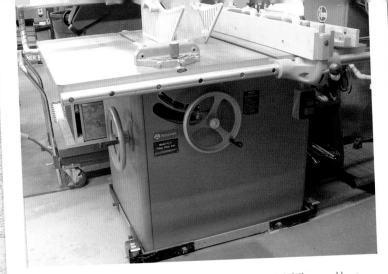

This 1970s Rockwell 12/14 table saw weighs 800 lbs. and has a 5hp, 3-phase motor to handle any job you can throw at it. 12" blades are standard, but a 14" blade is optional, allowing up to 5" cut depth. I keep this saw set up for rip cuts to complement the crosscut and dado functions of the Unisaws.

Cutting to length of rough stock and squaring of large panels is done at the 1968 16" Delta Rockwell turret radial arm saw. With a crosscut capacity of 24" and over 5" in depth, it's rare to find a project this saw can't handle. A second blade guard allows for the fitting of an 18" blade for any extreme jobs requiring up to 6" of depth! The fence has a sliding cutoff stop made up of a pair of aluminum T-tracks, which allows for repeatable cutoffs up to 6' in length. I acquired this already restored classic for $300 from a fellow who was just trying to clean out his storage shed.

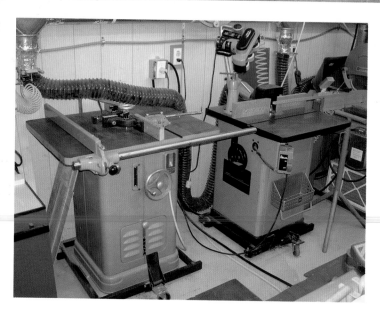

A pair of Delta HD spindle shapers, one vintage 1966 and one more modern fitted with a power feeder, allow for a variety of shaping tasks using 1/2", 3/4", 1" spindles and router bits. Mobile bases allow them to be moved back against the wall when not in use, and each is convenient to a gate for the dust collection system.

Large jointers are often joked about as being aircraft carriers, with their wide, flat tops. At 8' long and 1,700 pounds., this certainly holds true for this vintage 16" Moak jointer with a 5 hp direct drive motor. The three-toed design is often seen on old industrial jointers, as the three points always result in the machine sitting flat on the floor rather than possibly rocking on four feet. The other advantage of the single rear foot is that it provides the operator with more standing room and foot clearance when operating the machine.

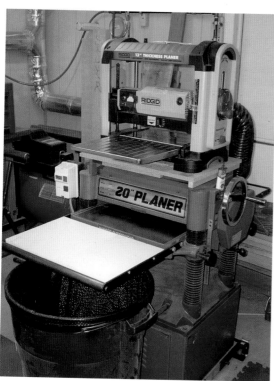

By piggybacking a bench top planer on top of a bigger, stationary machine I get a compact planing station that can handle heavy-duty dimensioning as well as fine finishing cuts. They share the same dust collection hose, which can quickly be switched back and forth.

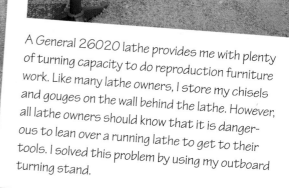

A General 26020 lathe provides me with plenty of turning capacity to do reproduction furniture work. Like many lathe owners, I store my chisels and gouges on the wall behind the lathe. However, all lathe owners should know that it is dangerous to lean over a running lathe to get to their tools. I solved this problem by using my outboard turning stand.

A TOUR OF JOHN LANNOM'S SHOP

Loveland, OH

it's five o'clock somewhere

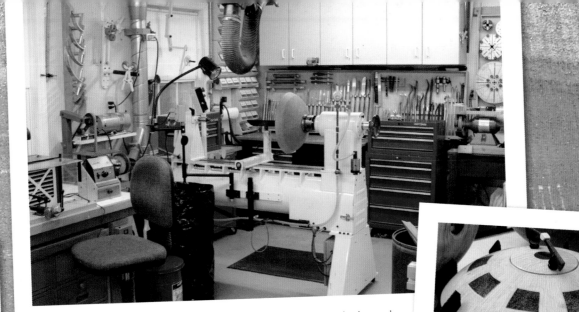

The left hand corner of the shop houses my 2436 Oneway lathe and all necessary tools on the wall behind and in wall cabinets. At the right is a picture of a piece I am working on for a Guild contest. The Ohio Valley Woodturners Guild has two contest each year. This contest features "Elevated Turnings".

As a small child I would sit for hours and watch my dad build furniture in his home shop. He furnished most of our home from that small backyard shop. He kept it locked when he was away, but I would climb in the window and "play" with his tools. It was many years later when I told him of my escapades. I guess that started my interest in woodworking, taking classes in high school and college. I've had shops in the garage and basement and finally in 1995 after my retirement, I built this space at the rear of my property. It is 24' square with a vacuum closet room projecting outside those dimensions. I discovered green wood turning about ten years ago. I now do very little "squarallel" (as I call it) work; only when my wife Carole demands it.

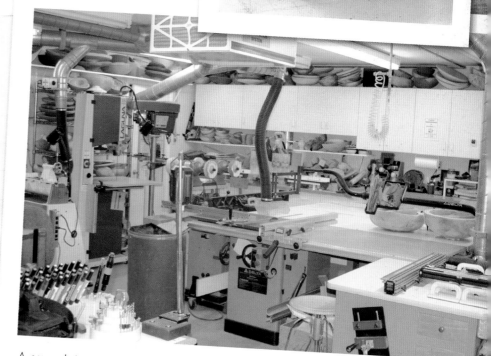

A general view of the rear wall of the shop. I have wall and floor cabinets along the entire wall for storage. A 10" cabinet saw with large outfeed table which also serves as a build/assembly surface but takes up quite a bit of space.

My surface decoration workstation. Here I can mount my turnings on a carving vise and get to any surface using a comfortable work position. I carve, burn and color here. Notice the dust collection unit immediately behind the work area. All necessary tools are stored underneath. The drawer section rolls out revealing another movable work surface.

A picture of my router table with vac attachment and storage in drawers and underneath. This work surface is at the same height as the cabinet saw and serves as additional support when sawing large sheet goods.

My cyclone vacuum system in its own separate room. It is piped to all stationary machines using spiral pipe and waste gates. At top is my four stage buffing station utilizing two Baldor buffing motors. This is used for buffing out high gloss finishes on some of my work.

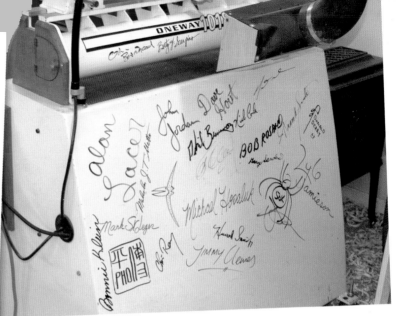

My small 1018 Oneway lathe (front at left) used for small detail work. Notice all the signatures on the front of the base. These are turners from all over the country that we invite to demonstrate for our Guild. Part of my duties as Vice President is to host and house them while they are visiting. I have them sign the lathe. Kinda like Willie Nelson's guitar.

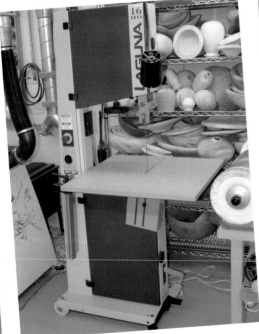

My 16HD Laguna band saw used mostly for rounding out turning blanks. It is fitted with ceramic guides and a 3/8"-wide set 3tpi for sawing greenwood.

Chop saw station with vac connections. Like most woodworkers, I never throw away any of my cut-off giblets. Piled in the rear are some of mine. There must be a project just around the corner that will require them.

A TOUR OF DICK HARBEN'S SHOP Lafayette, IN

With five adult children and five grandchildren, It's easy to find a project to work on. The Hall Tree/Bench (at right) was made for my son. He will finish it and add the mirrors and coat hooks.

Me with a back hoe I made. You can also see a hall tree/bench peeking over my shoulder. At top left is another project, a doll's cradle.

Probably not the shop you would expect, but I live in a condo without a whole lot of space and the garage is open to other neighbors. So I simply put my shop in the 12' x 15' spare bedroom. Nice pink curtains, huh? It holds a Shopsmith, band saw, small jointer and thickness planer. I was in a hurry to move my shop from my house to the condo and I didn't take time to take down the pink curtains. This shop lasted about 1 1/2 years until I found the garage I'm in now.

My magazines, Skil saw, routers, sanders, etc. were stored on the back wall above the Shopsmith.

I retired from a lighting manufacturing company in Fishers, IN in Jan. of 2007 as a project engineer. After watching woodworking shows on TV and reading a lot of wood books, my goal when I retired was to have a woodworking shop.

Now that I'm retired I figured you need to stay active to keep healthy. So I start my day walking two to three miles around the mall, go to breakfast, chat with some other retires and about 9 am go to my shop until 5 PM, just like a job. But now I'm the boss. Anyone that is in the area and would like to visit, give me a call. I'm the only Harben in the Lafayette phone book.

When I retired in January, 2005, I found a 24' x 30' garage to rent that had been the office/model for a garage builder who went out of business. It has two rooms just under 15' x 24'. The main room is carpeted in a tight weave pattern, so I have no problem moving equipment around. It's also easy on your feet, and I have no problem keeping it clean since the owner left a vacuum behind.

Since part of the shop is carpeted. I vacuum before I leave unless I'm in a middle of a big cutting project. It would only get messed up again.

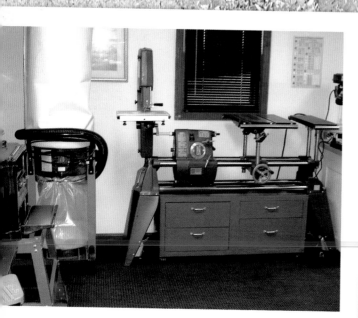

Since this photo was taken, I made my band saw a stand-alone tool, since it's a tool I use a great deal.

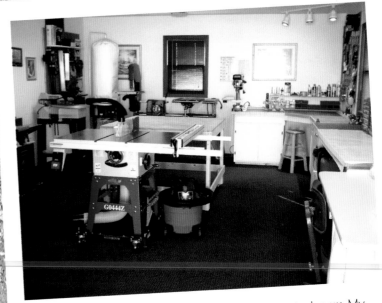

As you walk into the front door you enter the carpeted room. My jointer and planer are against the wall on the left, with my table saw placed in the center of the room. My working "desk" is in the corner on the right, with other counter space.

Immediately to the left of the front door is my desk and my library of over 180 woodworking books, most from the Woodworker's Book Club! Actually, the books have recently been moved into the library (bathroom) to make way for a TV and VCR.

A couple of other projects. On the left, one of five rocking horses I made, and above is part of a set of play kitchen cabinets I made for my grandson's nursery school. The hutch and refrigerator aren't shown.

As you walk into the second (uncarpeted) room and turn immediately to the left, my radial arm saw (with dedicated shop vacuum) sits at the ready. My miter saw sits on the bench beyond the radial arm.

I've added a switch to the front of my radial arm saw for the vacuum. This makes turning on the vacuum a little more convenient.

As the magazine library behind the radial arm saw (see above) has grown I added a shower curtain to keep the dust off them.

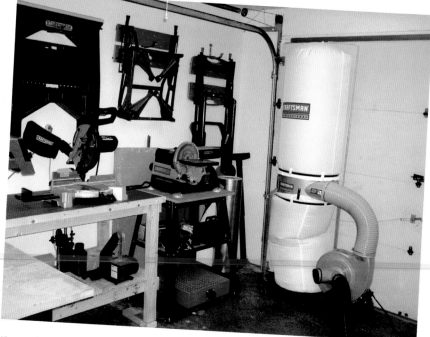

From the picture at the top of the page, if you turn to your right you can see my disc/belt sander, 1 1/2 hp dust collector and the overhead door for moving larger items in and out of the shop.

Lumber storage is located to the right of the overhead door (easier in-and-out). The planer is moved from room to room to be close to the wood supply on big jobs. I found that low cost plastic garden hose storage racks work well for dust collection hoses as well.

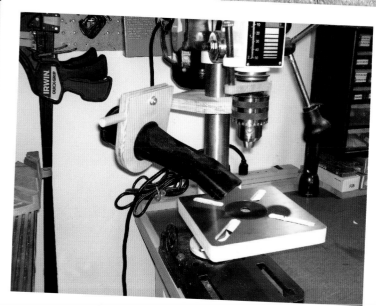

A couple of clever things in the shop that I'm proud of. At left I installed a roll of commercial wrapping paper under my table saw's outfeed table. I pull it over the top of the table when I'm painting a project. Above you see a directional dust pickup for my drill press. Keeps the dust out of the way so I can see what I'm doing.

I am 32 years old, married with two children. I have been in the carpentry/construction industry for 15 years. For the past five years I have been working full time as a building inspector for the City of Holland. Prior to that I built and remodeled houses. In addition to a side job here or there — working on rental properties and spending what little free time I have in my shop — I have made many pieces for the City during the slow winter months. Many of these pieces can be seen in City Hall. Most of the lumber I use I mill with an Alaskan sawmill, let air dry and plane and finish in my shop. My father was a carpenter also, specializing in repairing and rebuilding pipe organs. He was always very proud of his shop in the basement of our house. I inherited his tools when he died 17 years ago. I have since taken the shop concept to a new level. I built my 800+ square foot shop (attached to the rear of my house) over two years ago. It has a cathedral ceiling with exposed collar ties, many windows and is fully insulated and drywalled. In addition, it has its own electrical sub-panel, furnace w/central air, wood stove and 4' crawl space.

From the outside you can see that one side of my shop opens to our deck. Notice the 100' black cherry tree that has more than 20' of straight clear trunk which are all over our property.

A TOUR OF
ERIC DAVIS'
SHOP Holland, MI

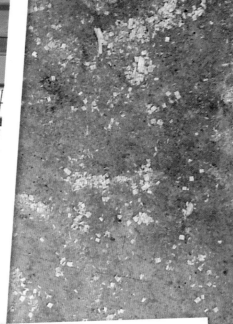

This 3hp table saw will cut anything, even fingers, OUCH! I made the outfeed table on heavy-duty drawer slides so that it slides out of the way of the miter gauge or for long lumber.

My shop is part of our house. I designed it so that it could easily be turned into living space for resale.

I have a few pieces of lumber on this rack, but I have been stock piling rough sawn lumber (that I have harvested), in a different garage.

My father made this disc sander (at front) out of a washing machine motor 25 years ago. It is one of my favorite tools.

French doors open to the side of my house where I can back my truck up, level with the floor of the shop.

The door in the back leads to our laundry room, where my daughter Eli stands wondering what I am taking pictures of.

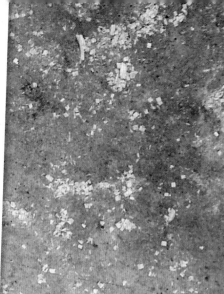

Looking down from the top, these double 2x8 collar ties are structural. They are handy for hanging things from or storing lumber.

I built this 4' x 7' maple top work bench last winter. I find that there is no such thing as too much table space.

In case you are wondering why everything is so clean — I cleaned for these pictures — or did I take picture because it was clean? Either way, this is rare, usually there is saw dust on everything and it is not nearly this neat.

A TOUR OF KEN JOHNSON'S SHOP

Lancaster, PA

Here I am holding the first dulcimer I ever made. It is made entirely of black walnut.

My shop sits on a concrete pad and is 12' x 16'. I chose a barn style roof and had two lofts added for storage space. Since my floor plan was small, I needed all the overhead storage I could get for wood and tools. Due to limited access to my backyard the shed had to be pre-fabricated and assembled onsite.

When I was very young I spent a lot of time with my father in his workshop. As a boy I built countless projects with increasing difficulty which led up to the making of my first Appalachian dulcimer at the age of twelve. I always enjoyed the thought process that went into my projects and the feeling of satisfaction as I learned new skills and completed a project.

After I graduated from college and moved out on my own, I got into other hobbies as I had no place to do my woodworking. Even when I bought a house years later I didn't have an acceptable place to set up shop. The hassle of having to set up my tools in the backyard made it a rare occasion that I would build anything too elaborate.

After my father passed away three years ago, I decided to get back into woodworking. I built this workshop because of my love of woodworking and in memory of my father. Although it is small (12' x 16') it is extremely functional. I live in the city on a small piece of property, so size was an issue.

I built the cabinets and hand picked every piece of equipment to maximize space and to handle the type of projects I like to do. I have built projects ranging from picture frames to desk clocks to Appalachian dulcimers.

There are many other unique aspects of my shop that make it very functional and easy to work in. I have spent countless hours creating this workshop and now I have a place to escape to and do what I love most.

My bench is made out of 2x4s and a solid-core luan door. The construction is simple but it is sturdy and functional. I chose fluorescent lighting fixtures with electronic ballasts so I don't have to wait for my lights to warm up in cold weather. I even researched the best bulbs to use and went with daylight bulbs rated at around 5000K. These are close to natural sunlight and don't distort your perception of colors, which is important when staining. I also had an extra window added above my bench for natural lighting and a better view.

Keith Johnson Jr.
1935 - 2004

This workshop and all that I create here, I dedicate to the memory of my Father, Keith Johnson Jr., for teaching me the art of woodworking. His love and kindness have made me who I am today, and a part of him will live on in all that my hands create.

Kenneth S. Johnson

After my shop was completed, I framed this plaque and photo and dedicated my shop to the memory of my father. He taught me everything I know.

The shop is wired for 50 amps, with 22 outlets on four separate circuits for lighting, machinery, dust collection and air cleaning. I insulated the walls with R13 insulation and put up 1/2" plywood to panel the walls. With a 5000btu window air conditioner and two 5000btu electric heaters I can stay comfortable all year long.

Above my Ridgid contractor's saw hang four cabinets which I built. They hang on a beveled cleat that wraps around my shop so I can easily relocate them if I need to. I designed them to utilize two sheets of birch plywood, one 1/2" sheet and one 3/4" sheet. Including hinges and hardware I built all four for around $100. I should have made four more. You can never have enough storage.

My Jet midi-lathe (sitting on the floor) is awaiting it's new home. In the corner is my Rockwell 32" radial drill press. It has a mortising attachment, and I also use it as a vertical drum sander. You should also take note of my most important piece of equipment; my 5-speaker surround-sound tuner (compliments of my friend Andy). No shop is complete without one.

The cabinets all have adjustable shelves for maximum utilization. I drilled a hole in the back of this cabinet for running the cord to my cordless drill's battery charger.

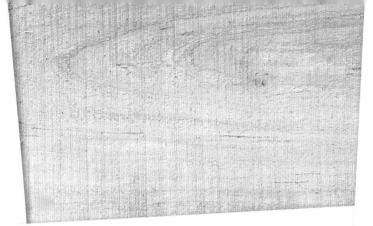

I keep my Craftsman 6" jointer on wheels so I can roll it out of the corner when I need it. It is an early 1950s model that I got at a sale for $250. I like buying old equipment like this because it is very heavy duty and easy to repair. You couldn't find a new jointer of this quality for that kind of price.

This corner of my shop is mainly for wood storage. I plan to build a wall-mounted lathe bench under the window with storage underneath for my miscellaneous wood. Here you can see a bench/shoe rack, that I made for my wife Wendy, in its final stages. I also made a matching piece that stands upright for her to set her jewelry box on. Did I mention that piece holds shoes too? The piece in the corner is a horizontal drum sander that my father built. His many machine patents hang above the doors.

The loft over my bench is used mainly for small power tools and my nail guns. You can see my Porter Cable pancake compressor on the left. On the ceiling I have a 50' air hose reel and a JDS 750-ER air cleaner which keeps the dust out of the air. It may be a bit over-sized for my shop, but it does a great job.

A TOUR OF GARY LYTTON'S SHOP

Charleston, SC

GARY'S WOODSHOP

An exterior view of my shop. Being the builder of both the adjacent house and shop, it was easy to make sure the brick and designs matched.

Interior shot of the shop showing the wood storage system I built and several pieces of equipment. The long wood beam hanging from the ceiling is the "strongback" I used to build the cedar boat.

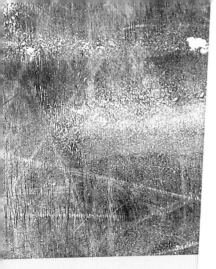

I am 56 years old, married for 32 years to the love of my life and have two grown children. I am a home builder by trade, but have been woodworking for about 30 years. I actually started woodworking when my children were very small. I was an avid golfer, but I worked 60+ hours a week. I didn't think it right to be gone all week and then leave again on Saturday to play golf, so I started woodworking because I could do it in short stints at the house. I call it my therapy and it truly is my way to relax. I have built many different things over the past thirty years, but mostly I have built furniture out of cherry, walnut, oak, mahogany, etc. The past couple of years, I have branched out somewhat. My most recent project was a cedar boat and I am now studying relief carving. I hope to place some future carvings on my furniture pieces.

The shop is almost two years old now. We relocated from Charlotte, NC two years ago and I reproduced the shop I had there. It is 24' x 30' or 720sf. It is fully insulated, heated and air-conditioned, but I rarely use either. The insulation keeps it comfortable most of the time. The numerous windows also provide excellent cross ventilation as well as an abundance of light. It also has a LCD TV mounted near the ceiling in one corner. Now I can continue my woodworking even during football season.

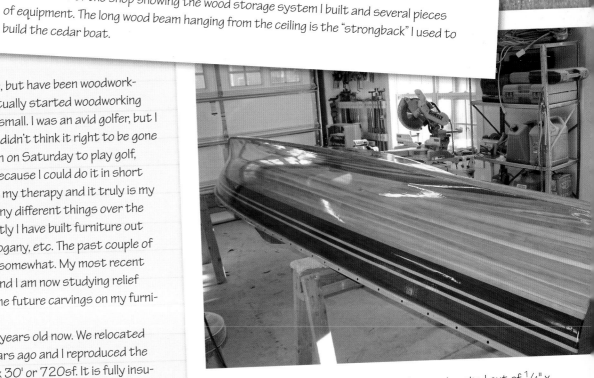

My most recent project. This 17' boat is constructed out of $1/4''$ x $1''$ beveled cedar strips. Once the cedar strips are in place, several coats of epoxy followed by several coats of marine varnish are applied. It was a most enjoyable project. The boat, nearing completion, is still turned upside down.

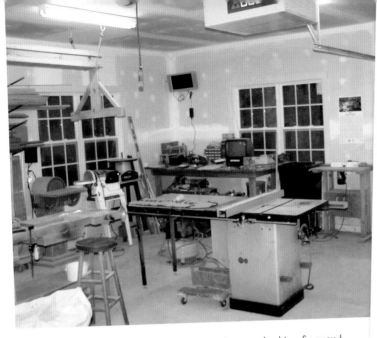

A shot of the shop interior taken from the rear looking forward.

A hand operated drill press. It was manufactured in 1902. It is built out of cast iron and weighs 72lbs.

This Shopsmith is 30+ years old. It is the first piece of equipment I purchased when I started woodworking in my garage. I still use it for lathe work and as a drill press. It is a great piece of equipment.

"The size of a persons shop, the finest tools that money can buy and the best raw materials that one starts with do not, most of the time, produce quality, fine craftsmanship, works of art or help in creating or making wooden items. What does though, is passion (not love), heart, soul, ingenuity and a lot of homemade jigs!"
–Johnny W Morlan

Clamp storage system I built using 2x4s as spacers.

Disc sander I built using an electric motor from an old washing machine. The disk came from the Shopsmith kit I started woodworking with 30 years ago.
It works quite well.

Some antique tools I have acquired. I enjoy collecting old tools.
My next project is a storage cabinet for my hand tools.

A grandfather clock I built two years ago out of walnut.

A TOUR OF BOB BONNER'S SHOP El Paso, TX

Bob's Shop is a metal building 30' x 30' x 12' with four windows, four skylights, refrigerated AC and gas heating.

This photo shows the overall layout of the shop.

I am 75 years old and have dreamed of having the shop that I now have. I developed an interest in woodworking in high school and have been making things from that time until now. I love woodturning and furniture making. The machines in this shop allow me to make some very nice items.

The dinette table top is 5'2" across from tip to tip. The center piece is laminate with bubinga pattern. The light colored strips between the segments are of birds-eye maple. The inner segments are of lyptus wood. The middle segments are of kingwood and the outer segments are of Honduran mahogany. The pedestal is 5" in diameter and made of kingwood. The feet on the pedestal are of Honduran mahogany.

This is another view of the shop showing the 14" band saw with 6" riser in the foreground. The lathe caddy with tools and sharpening system is beside the lathe which is just behind the band saw.

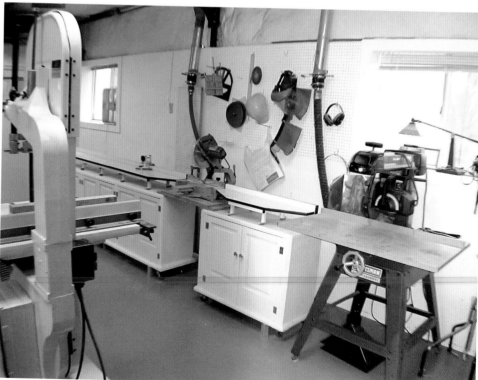

The crosscutting area incorporates the 10" sliding compound miter saw with the radial arm saw system to allow the crosscutting of boards up to 24' long or longer if the door is open.

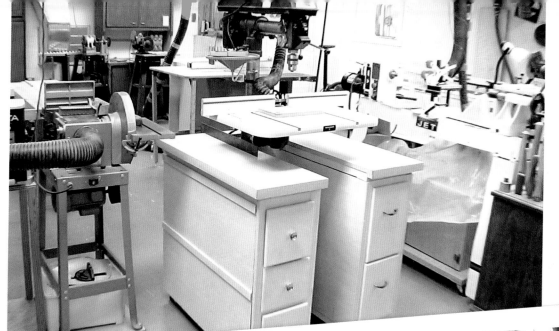

I designed and built the mobile drill press accessory cabinet. It can be moved back so the platform on the radial drill press can be lowered.

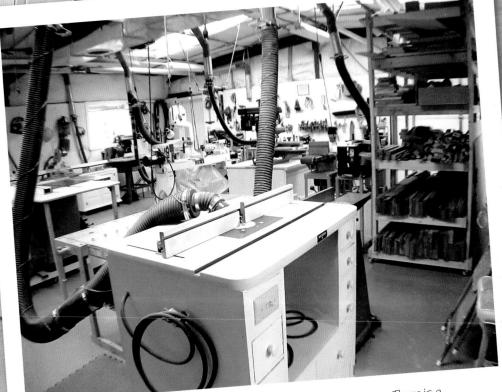

The router table has lots of storage for bits, routers and accessories. There is a portable oscillating spindle sander stored here that can be mounted in the table for a large sanding platform. Note the extra height so I don't have to bend over. This system is also mobile.

The large storage rack for wood is 8'H x 3'W x 7'L. It can hold a lot of wood.

I made this shroud to enclose the lathe. Made from PVC pipe frame with shower curtains surrounding, it serves to contain the flying chips which previously would fly everywhere. Up above, you can peek through the curtain and see me working at the lathe.

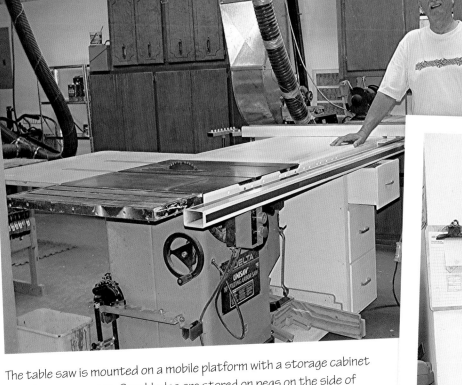

The table saw is mounted on a mobile platform with a storage cabinet on it for accessories. Saw blades are stored on pegs on the side of the cabinet. 4' x 8' sheets are handled easily with this system.

The air compressor, which is connected to an auto-retracting hose reel mounted overhead in the center of the shop, is enclosed in an insulated closet with the dust collection system to cut down on the noise in the shop. The two-stage dust collection system is connected to all machines in the shop.

Not too bad for an old horse barn! The building is 24' x 36'. Lots of storage in the old hay loft.

A TOUR OF MILTON IPPOLITO'S SHOP Wampum, PA

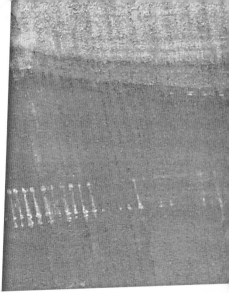

The shop is a remodeled pole barn. It's insulated very well and is heated with an electric furnace and heat pump.

My name is Milton Ippolito, I'm 60 years old, I've always been an avid do-it-yourself guy, so when I retired from the military after almost 27 years, I started working on my shop. It was an old horse barn built some 25 years back. I renovated it both inside and out and started buying the machines and tools I needed (wanted) to get started. My plan was to build kitchen cabinets, but before I could get started on my wife's new kitchen, our daughter announced she was pregnant, so of course I started building baby furniture. The baby furniture was a labor of love (the boys are 27 months now and they love the beds I built for them).

The shop is 24' x 36' with an 8' x 9' overhead door, I installed the basics, planer, jointer, table saw, band saw and so on. The shop is small but functional. When the lawn tractors are outside there is ample room to maneuver sheet goods.

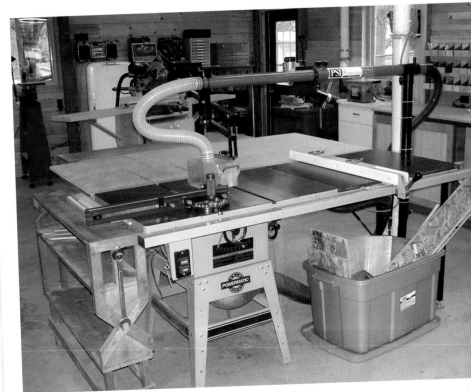

The table saw occupies the center of the space.

97

This was just after I completed the collection system to each machine. I used low-voltage switch gates at each location.

Got that old Craftsman lathe from a neighbor for fixing a table. Note the drill bit cabinet to the left of the bathroom door. And, of course, the short stock storage located over the jointer.

The router table was Norm's design. I purchased the plan and video. It turned out great!

"I've been working on this shop in my head for the about 30 years give or take. The Shop still is not really done and maybe it never will be. There is always room for improvement in any Shop — so you just keep working..."

Here's a good shot of the outfeed table on the table saw. Cabinetmaker's bench fits nicely under the lip.

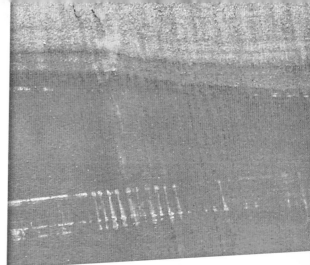

This is probably the best thing anyone could ever do to a miter saw. Got the plan from *Popular Woodworking* magazine.

Just finished the doors for the main bench. Note the built-in radial arm saw. Works well. I told my wife if she wanted quality cabinets and beautiful doors I had to have a few fixtures for the shop before I started. (I was right, wasn't I)??

The covered front porch is 5' wide and is decked with pressure treated wood. The stairs at the North end of the porch lead to the cabin.

A TOUR OF GEORGE WEISNER'S SHOP

Sister Bay, WI

The building is 64' long x 27' wide, built on a slab. Non-heated garage. The half-bath and work shop are set up with radiant floor heating. The back wall is bermed into the ground three feet and is only 6' high inside the building, in an attempt to reduce the height of the structure as viewed from the cabin.

I've been married for 38 years with two children and four grand children. I retired from teaching machine shop at Conant High School, in Illinois, after 33 years. I built this shop to build furniture and restore prewar pin ball games. I am fascinated with Shaker furniture and oval boxes. We built our 1800 sq. ft. dream cabin (and my shop) preparing for a comfortable retirement in Sister Bay, WI. That worked well until my wife decided she was too far from the grandchildren. So the dream house and shop are for sale, and we've now moved to Spring Grove, IL where I get to do it all again!

The South wall of the shop with my bench (for contemplating the next project) and great windows for letting in light (and controlling the temperature). The front wall is made from 5x7 oak logs that were left over from the adjacent cabin on the property.

I love this tool cabinet. It's made from recycled quarter-sawn fir bleacher seats. I built it after a design I found in a copy of *Shop Notes*. The cabinet is used to store common layout and bench tools. It's close, convenient and easy to relocate.

I didn't get to add a central dust collection system, central compressed air, a wood stove and about half a dozen other things —next shop.

My intention was to sand and finish the interior of the log wall, the effect is really striking. All of the windows were recycled from various remodel jobs that I helped friends with.

Looking West are my trusty planer and jointer. Through the double doors is the garage. The front door and double doors between the workshop and garage were built on site.

The half-bath and workshop are set up with radiant floor heating, making it very comfortable to work in the shop in the colder months.

The building is oriented south so the summer sun is limited, but the winter sun fills the workshop with a warm glow.

The rear wall (only 6' high) is a perfect place for a machine bench and storage unit. From left to right on top are spots for a mortise machine, chop box and 12" finish planer. On the bottom, left to right, pull out shelves for hardware and jigs, roller for mechanic tools, spot for short cut-offs, roller for cutters, drills, router bits and machine accessories, four large and deep draws for power tools.

This is what I refer to as my Clamp Tower. It holds mostly good-old pipe clamps (they keep working!). There's also some new fast-acting clamps and more. It's on wheels so it travels to the work. No lugging clamps around.

Custom trusses and beams were used for the roof system so no exposed support posts are used. Turning left from the photo above you see the East wall. These photos were taken during move-out, so it looks a little bare. Sigh.

A nice pile of quarter-sawn oak waiting for a project. Logs:Free. Mill cost: $60. The results:Priceless. 95% clear and straight lumber!

A lumber rack is located on the west wall of the garage. Simple 2x4 arms with ³/4" plywood gussets and end caps are screwed to the studs, easily changed as needs change. Something I learned as a shop teacher, a facility needs to change as needs change, don't make anything to permanent.

If the shop looks a bit empty, it's because some of the tools have been moved: A Grizzly 1¹/2 hp shaper; 10" Craftsman radial arm saw; 12" Dewalt finish planer; 12" Craftsman molder planner; Delta mortiser; Grizzly combination belt sander/ buffer; Grizzly scroll saw and some other tools.

A TOUR OF RAY MERRELL'S SHOP

Pueblo, CO

My shop is unique in that it is in a round building! The structure itself is a thin shell concrete covered by 3" of polyurethane foam that provides an equivalent of an R65 insulation without any breaks. Having concrete on the inside provides the thermal mass to retain an even temperature. Thin shell concrete structures can withstand hurricanes, tornadoes, earthquakes and termites hate them, plus they are fireproof!

The shop is part of the larger complex of seven domes. Three for the house, one for the open air patio and the final three are the two garages and the shop. The shop is attached to the two-car garage, has a double door leading into it to facilitate moving large objects in and out of the shop, and allows for expansion of the work area into one garage bay if necessary.

I began woodworking when I was a kid. The high school architecture and wood classes helped a lot in my abilities to create things out of wood. Living in an old house for 40 years certainly challenged my creativity. I have never had a dedicated place for my hobby until we retired and moved to Colorado. Being able to create our own home design, it included my 32' dome shop! Needless to say the curved walls of the domes are very challenging when placing things against them. Woodworking is a rewarding and beneficial hobby that I continue to enjoy daily now! I continue to make a lot of sawdust as I strive to hone my woodworking skills.

Being a dome there is an abundance of storage against the curved walls without interfering with the work area. A side view of the shelves illustrates the depth of the bottom area versus that of the top shelves. Tops are about 8" deep but I can store almost two five-gallon buckets underneath them.

As we built it, we installed our 6" PVC vacuum pipe underground. This keeps it out of the way and provides a good earth ground as well. There are two inputs in the floor and one through the garage/shop wall. We installed radiant heating with its own thermostat so I can regulate the temperature in the winter. The Pex heating tubes and the power and vacuum port are shown here stubbed up. The floor is ready for cement!

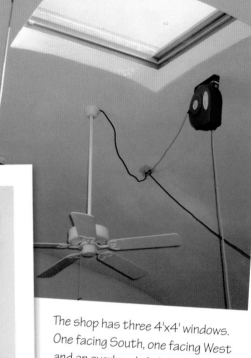

The shop has three 4'x4' windows. One facing South, one facing West and an overhead skylight. All open for fresh air. I added a ceiling fan and two 4' fluorescent fixtures to help illuminate the shop. The ceiling of the dome is 14' high, so there is plenty of room to turn over an 8' board without worrying about bringing down the ceiling!

To have some mobility I build a clamp rack that can be moved to the project. In the right corner of the west wall next to the maple topped 6' worktable. Also illustrated is the second flat wall separating the shop from the garage where I have my note board of future project and the wife's wish list.

Besides the maple-topped table, I also have a work table 36" x 74" with a metal vise on one end and a 3' wood vise on the other end. This is great for glue up and assembly.

In the center of the shop is the Grizzly G1023SLX table saw with additional storage under the table extension. These bins are great for storing lots of saw blades, sandpaper for different sanders and, other miscellaneous stuff. At the rear of the saw is another extension (shown at left) that folds up to add useful floor space. I also added rubberized floor pads that help relieve the stress of standing on concrete for long periods of time.

One challenge I faced was creating blast gates that fit onto PVC pipes. They are not available commercially, but I made it work using PVC toilet traps. I sandwiched a $3/4$" piece of MDF between the two after coping out a 4" curved opening. Two $3/4$" plywood gates (at left) — one blocking the 4" pipe and one allowing the airflow, make it all work. Painting the handles red & green make it obvious whether the gate is open or not.

Attach the flexible hose to one end and mount the assembly into the floor pipe and it's ready to go!

I have built mobile bases for my Makita LS1013 dual-slide compound 10" miter saw. In this picture I left the removable handles on to show how easily they can be relocated. Kind of like a wheel barrel moving it around.

Storage is always a big thing in a shop and I have a unique drawer tool storage system. I have labeled each drawer so I know where to find tools.

A custom pine bookcase for a friend.

The butler below also has a matching French maid that holds a towel. Both designs were reworked for "bathroom" duty.

Some projects are just for fun! My wife and I decided to make this for our visitor's powder room. Notice the top hat? It actually covers the extra roll of toilet paper and was the hardest part.

Custom shelves of alder for a neighbor.

A TOUR OF DOUG LEONARD'S SHOP

Urbandale, IA

My shop is 24' x 30' with a square missing in one corner. It's L-shaped to comply with the Urbandale building code. My wife, Janis, landscaped the shop.

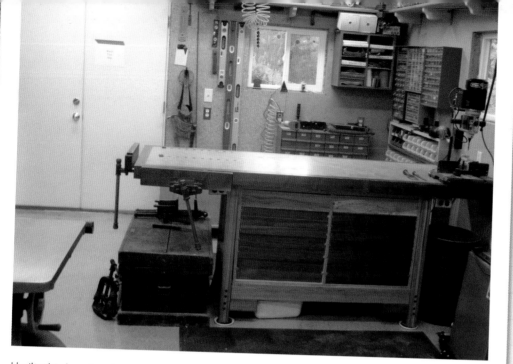

This is Rusty. He is one of the shop cats and is 16 (human) years old. He still makes it out to the shop every day to help me out.

I built this bench using walnut, red oak and birch ply. It is all mortise and tenon with pegs going through the joints. The only screws are in the vises and the electrical outlets. The old tool box is my great-grandfather's, handed down to me. The antique tools on the shelf above the window came out of the tool box, including a Stanley #45 plane.

I had been using a double garage as my shop until last year when I was married. I had to make room for my wife to park, so in July of 2005 I started thinking of building a shop. I called around to get estimates. If the person showed up, they never followed through with giving me an estimate. One place finally came through with a "rough" estimate, which I thought was extremely high. I thought, "forget that idea". I sat down and designed a shop with what I would like. I've spent a year building my new shop, and I'm doing the finishing touches now. I did 85% of the work myself. My life-long friends helped with what I could not do myself. I built a small room for the dust collector, air compressor and the main electrical box. I also did all the wiring. I have 16 fluorescent lights, 28, 110-volt outlets, 5, 220-volt outlets and outside security lights. I have storage in the attic, that has a fold-up ladder, for wood and jigs. I ran a gas pipe for an overhead heater during the winter. I live in the city so had to go by the code.

As you can see, this wall is my storage area for a variety of clamp styles.

Early stages of moving in. You can see a miter saw, table saw, workbench, grinder and my grandfather's antique tools on the window shelf.

The dust collection and wiring for all 220-volt machines is in-ground. After doing the forms, I laid out the PVC for the dust collection and wiring. Then had a concrete pumper truck bring in the cement.

My wife and I are currently looking for some land in the country to build a house and a Morton building for my shop.

A small desk area includes a TV, stereo, phone, clock, file cabinet and note-book of plans and a special photo of Sam Maloof and myself. It was taken August of 2006 at the Anderson Ranch while I was taking a seminar that Sam put on for the weekend.

This is one of my lumber storage areas. It's built with 2x4s sandwiched between 1x4s, which are screwed into the studs using lag bolts. Directly above is a heater that heats my solar collector on cloudy and/or cold days.

One of the highlights of my life was meeting Sam Maloof. He is a very humble person, a true inspiration and his ways sure influence ones' woodworking.

I used dadoes, mortise and tenons and a some lathe work to construct this walnut display cabinet.

115

A TOUR OF THOM RITTER'S SHOP Seattle, WA

It's a nice playhouse, I spent $20,000 on it, got everything my way and on my schedule. It's 24' x 40', so I have plenty of room to work in front of the car and other rigs.

I'm a 51 year old fire department mechanic. We're just across Puget Sound from Seattle. My wife and I live on 2½ acres and we like working in the yard. This garage is the first structure I've ever built, except for a garden shed kit. I have a carpenter buddy who gave me lots of coaching. "Get it as straight and plumb and square as you can." I borrowed a framing nailer. The only part I farmed out was the garage doors. They had 'em up in four hours. It could have taken me days. It took me about 30-35 eight-hour days to complete the garage.

My "playhouse" turned out better than my wildest dreams. I never had a single argument with a contractor but I did have a few discussions with the "superintendent". I explained to her what I had in mind — I've been designing this garage in my mind since we bought the lot in 1998. I have a separate propane tank for the garage and a 50-gallon gas water heater to heat the floor. I have about $1,400 in the radiant floor system. It's awesome. I've settled on 60° as the best temperature for working. It's even heat, end to end, bottom to top. The radiant heat means no blowing sawdust around the shop.

It's about as big a building that one guy can do on his own. I had help with the slab, standing up the walls and standing up the trusses. I only shot myself with the framing nailer twice — neither was serious. I framed the whole thing with my Porter Cable, 19.2 volt saw/drill combo. It was nice not having to deal with a power cord.

I love motorsports and always wanted to do a floor like this. I thought my wife would think it was a dumb idea. As I was nearing completion, she said, "I don't want to have a boring gray floor. How about we paint it, and let's do the checkered flag thing." I couldn't believe my ears. I said, "Honey, that's a great idea!"

Construction, clockwise from top: Days 1-5. Digging the foundation — our county regulations call for a thickened perimeter — I didn't plan ahead. I dug the perimeter, then realized I had to dig the middle portion down 6" for the slab. Days 8-9. Laying the tubing for the radiant floor. 750 feet of tubing and three 250-foot loops. The junction box for the tubing is in the corner and the manifolds are mounted in a plywood box. The concrete is poured around it. Day 10. I invited a few buddies over to help me pour the slab. I provided lunch and cold beer afterwards. Day 12. Standing the walls up. Day 15. Sheathing the walls. I used plywood for the entire project — no OSB. The cost difference was only about $200. Day 22. The finished metal roof. I only fell off once. Luckily I didn't fall on the side with the rockery. I went over the edge feet first and was able to guide myself over the edge, hit the bank side and roll and only hurt my pride.

I decide to build myself a router table that has plenty of storage. I learned about book-matching the drawer fronts, and how steep the learning curve is when building drawers.

I found a woodworking bench plan in one of the magazines, using laminated plywood for the legs, with a mortise and tenon type joint for the stringers. A plywood piece at each end between the legs adds stability. The top is made of one sheet of $3/4$" melamine and one sheet of $3/4$" plywood laminated with screws. I drilled $3/4$" holes in the top for bench dogs. The bench is rock-solid.

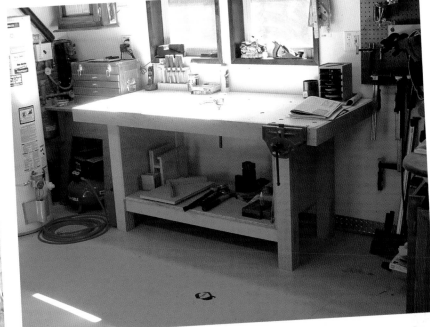

My father-in-law was a lifetime mechanic like myself. After he passed, I got some of the equipment from his garage. This chainfall comes in pretty handy. The I-beam he had was too short, so I asked around, and one of our volunteer Captains at work had four I-beams in his yard. Free is good.

The radiant floor system is awesome. I got most of the equipment from the Radiant Floor Company in Vermont, they cater to DIYers, a great company to deal with. I used a 50-gallon gas water heater, hooked to a 125-gallon, upright tank behind the shop. It works great, as there is only about 20 gallons of water in the floor tubing. I keep the thermostat set to 60-65°, that's a good temperature when working in the shop. (My wife loves getting in a nice warm car in the winter.) I think I spent around $400 on propane last winter.

By using attic trusses I have a clear space of 8' x 40' with 6' headroom at the peak. The truss builder says they will support 40 pounds per square foot. That's 3,200 lbs of junk! I don't plan on loading it that heavy, but this sure beats crawling around under the house. I used a pull-down attic step for access.

We painted the floor at the shop end tan. Wendy found some tool stencils at a craft store. Just to the left of the hammer is a ball cap. There's three of those — she painted our names and her parrot's name in these caps.

We do some silk-screening, shirts etc. so I built a dedicated work area for that. The device on the bench that looks like a drill press is actually a pad printer that can print logos on pens, mugs, golf balls, etc. All of the supplies fit in the cabinets, away from sawdust.

A guy has to have a place for some wood, I usually move Wendy's car out when I'm picking through it. Don't want to have an accident on the car! I think I need a better rack for sheet goods. I built a 2' x 2' x 2' box with wheels for small scraps. It's overflowing. Time to donate some to the woodstove.

The main shop is a copy of a 17th century English barn. It has 1,000 sq. ft. on the first floor and 350 sq. ft. on the second floor loft. The smaller building is 400 sq. ft. and houses about 10,000 board feet of cherry, tiger maple, walnut and chestnut.

A TOUR OF LOU SANSONE'S SHOP
Windham County, CT

A rare, 16-speed Walker Turner radial arm drill press resides in the corner of the shop. Delta bought the design years ago and continued to produce this same drill press up to 2002 for the reasonable cost of $10,400.

A 1967 Mercedes Benz "404.1 Unimog" purchased direct from the Belgian Military. Rust free, with only 25,000 original miles. Considered to be the most capable light duty 4 wheel drive vehicle ever made (including the modern Hummer), and is capable of hauling 3,000 lbs.

I designed and built the shop myself, cutting down all the trees and sawing them up myself with the help of my son and brother about six years ago. The entire shop is hand planed oak timbers and completely pegged together. The shop has a number of interesting "old iron" machines as well as a new sliding table saw. I've been building furniture for more than a decade and specialize in 18th century American style furniture. My circa 1730 home makes an ideal showcase for pieces such as the 1780 tall case clock on the next page.

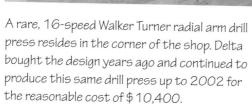

My vintage Moak Machinery 36" direct drive band saw is a work of beauty. It has a 24" resaw capacity and the 100% cast iron frame results in vibration free running. The 30 hp frame size, 5 hp 600 rpm super slow speed motor never feels a strain even with the toughest lumber.

The shop has a 28' clear span with 10' ceilings. Oneida industrial dust collection is used throughout the shop. The 1½"-thick hickory flooring is laid over insulation and also houses much of the electrical conduit that terminates in floor mounted boxes.

A single owner 37" x 75" Timesavers wide-belt sander really makes short work of processing highly figured lumber, which is a shop favorite. The 20 hp motor easily powers though any job.

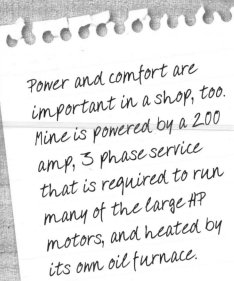

Power and comfort are important in a shop, too. Mine is powered by a 200 amp, 3 phase service that is required to run many of the large HP motors, and heated by its own oil furnace.

A three-legged , 5 hp, direct drive, 1946 Newman 60, 16" jointer has 24" wide cast iron tables that allow for easy skewing cuts on figured lumber. The mid 1980s, 24", Italian Casadie planer has four separate motors, the largest of which is the 12hp main drive motor.

The newest addition to the shop is the 2006 SCMI/Tecnomax S315 WS sliding table saw. It replaced a vintage Oliver 260 twin arbor sliding table saw. Ripping of rough lumber for a glue edge is easy work for this saw. Even large panels are easily squared with the sliding table and crosscut carriage.

The oldest machine is a early 1900s former pattern shop lathe that was originally driven by overhead leather belts. It has gone though a modernization upgrade and now sports a true four-speed gear box coupled to a 3 hp VFD type drive. It has a 20" inboard swing and 72" cc. Outboard turning is limited by the floor to spindle distance of 50"

A 1780 tall case clock is ready to be moved into its rightful home, located on the property.

125

SUPPLIERS

ADAMS & KENNEDY —
THE WOOD SOURCE
6178 Mitch Owen Rd.
P.O. Box 700
Manotick, ON
Canada K4M 1A6
613-822-6800
www.wood-source.com
Wood supply

ADJUSTABLE CLAMP COMPANY
404 N. Armour St.
Chicago, IL 60622
312-666-0640
www.adjustableclamp.com
Clamps and woodworking tools

B&Q
Portswood House
1 Hampshire Corporate Park
Chandlers Ford
Eastleigh
Hampshire, England SO53 3YX
0845 609 6688
www.diy.com
Woodworking tools, supplies and
hardware

BUSY BEE TOOLS
130 Great Gulf Dr.
Concord, ON
Canada L4K 5W1
1-800-461-2879
www.busybeetools.com
Woodworking tools and supplies

CRAFTSMAN PLANS
P.O. Box 325
Loveland, OH 45140
craftsmanplans.com
Plans, books, tools, hardware

CONSTANTINE'S WOOD CENTER
OF FLORIDA
1040 E. Oakland Park Blvd.
Fort Lauderdale, FL 33334
800-443-9667
www.constantines.com
Tools, woods, veneers, hardware

FRANK PAXTON LUMBER
COMPANY
5701 W. 66th St.
Chicago, IL 60638
800-323-2203
www.paxtonwood.com
Wood, hardware, tools, books

THE HOME DEPOT
2455 Paces Ferry Rd. NW
Atlanta, GA 30339
800-430-3376 (U.S.)
800-628-0525 (Canada)
www.homedepot.com
Woodworking tools, supplies and
hardware

KLINGSPOR ABRASIVES INC.
2555 Tate Blvd. SE
Hickory, N.C. 28602
800-645-5555
www.klingspor.com
Sandpaper of all kinds

LEE VALLEY TOOLS LTD.
P.O. Box 1780
Ogdensburg, NY 13669-6780
800-871-8158 (U.S.)
800-267-8767 (Canada)
www.leevalley.com
Woodworking tools and hardware

LEIGH INDUSTRIES LTD.
P.O. Box 357
104-1585 Broadway St.
Port Coquitlam, BC, Canada
V3C 4K6
800-663-8932
leighjigs.com
Tools and jigs

LIE-NIELSEN TOOLWORKS
Lie-Nielsen Toolworks
P.O. Box 9
Warren, ME 04864-0009
800-327-2520
lie-nielsen.com
handtools

LOWE'S COMPANIES, INC.
P.O. Box 1111
North Wilkesboro, NC 28656
800-445-6937
www.lowes.com
Woodworking tools, supplies and
hardware

ROCKLER WOODWORKING AND
HARDWARE
4365 Willow Dr.
Medina, MN 55340
800-279-4441
www.rockler.com
Woodworking tools, hardware and
books

TOOL TREND LTD.
140 Snow Blvd. Unit 1
Concord, ON
Canada L4K 4C1
416-663-8665
Woodworking tools and hardware

TREND MACHINERY & CUTTING
TOOLS LTD.
Odhams Trading Estate
St. Albans Rd.
Watford
Hertfordshire, U.K.
WD24 7TR
01923 224657
www.trendmachinery.co.uk
Woodworking tools and hardware

WATERLOX COATINGS
908 Meech Ave.
Cleveland, OH 44105
800-321-0377
www.waterlox.com
Finishing supplies

WHITECHAPEL LTD.
P.O. Box 11719
Jackson, WY 83002
800-468-5534
www.whitechapel-ltd.com
Fine quality hardware

WOODCRAFT SUPPLY LLC
1177 Rosemar Rd.
P.O. Box 1686
Parkersburg, WV 26102
800-535-4482
www.woodcraft.com
Woodworking hardware

WOODWORKER'S HARDWARE
P.O. Box 180
Sauk Rapids, MN 56379-0180
800-383-0130
www.wwhardware.com
Woodworking hardware

WOODWORKER'S SUPPLY
1108 N. Glenn Rd.
Casper, WY 82601
800-645-9292
http://woodworker.com
Woodworking tools and accessories,
finishing supplies, books and plans

THINK YOUR SHOP SHOULD HAVE BEEN IN THIS BOOK?

We don't disagree at all! We know that this book will stir many of you to look at your shop from a different point of view. If that view happens to be from behind a camera, then we'd like to share the view.

It's our expectation that the response to *Woodshop Lust* will be strong enough to offer another edition next year. If you'd like to have your shop considered for inclusion in a new edition, send a few sample photos and some brief information about yourself to:

David Thiel

Popular Woodworking Books

4700 East Galbraith Rd.

Cincinnati, OH 45236

or e-mail me at:

david.thiel@fwpubs.com

MORE GREAT TITLES FROM POPULAR WOODWORKING!

DAVID THIEL'S POWER TOOL MAINTENANCE

This is a comprehensive guide to cleaning, repairing and tuning up your woodworking power tools. You'll find an illustrated look at the functions and parts of each tool, tips on how to identify trouble spots and adjust parts to obtain optimal performance.

ISBN 13: 978-1-55870-755-9
ISBN 10: 1-55870-755-7
paperback, 128 p., #70708

HAND TOOL ESSENTIALS
From the editors of Popular Woodworking magazine

This book is about using hand tools in balance with your power tools to save you time, provide a more pleasant workworking experience and ultimately give you a better woodworking project. You'll learn how to choose and use hand tools for chopping, cutting, paring, sawing, marking, drilling and more.

ISBN 13: 978-1-55870-815-0
ISBN 10: 1-55870-815-4
paperback, 224 p., # Z0978

BUILDING WOODSHOP WORKSTATIONS
By Danny Proulx

Detailed plans are provided for:
- base-and wall-mounted cabinets
- a practical workbench
- miter saw workstation
- multifunctiion power tool cabinet
- power tool storage station
- mobile table saw center
- router table cabinet
- drill press center and more.

ISBN 13: 978-1-55870-637-8
ISBN 10: 1-55870-637-2
paperback, 128 p., #70585

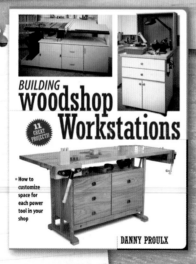

HOW TO DESIGN AND BUILD YOUR IDEAL WOODSHOP
By Bill Stankus

Plan your ideal woodshop — everything from lumber storage and ventilation to dust collection and lighting. Avoid potential mistakes and injuries with safety-first checklists. Make your workshop environment comfortable and cozy. Power and light your shop effectively. Learn how to consider your layout and budget issues.

ISBN 13: 978-1-55870-587-6
ISBN 10: 1-55870-587-2
paperback, 128 p., # 70522

These and other great woodworking books are available at your local bookstore, woodworking stores or from online suppliers.

www.popularwoodworking.com